EASE
INTO THE
BIBLE

EASE
INTO THE
BIBLE

How to Wade into the Water
of God's Word with Confidence

JEAN WILUND

B&H
PUBLISHING®
BRENTWOOD, TENNESSEE

Published by B&H Publishing Group
Brentwood, Tennessee

Dewey Decimal Classification: 220.07
Subject Heading: BIBLE—STUDY AND TEACHING
/ BIBLE—READING / BIBLE—USE

Cover design by B&H Publishing Group.
Illustration by Wayne Brezinka.

1 2 3 4 5 6 • 27 26 25 24

To Larry

Since the moment Steve, the *Harcombe Preacher*,
pronounced us "man and wife," you've prayed for me,
cared for me, protected me, and loved me well.

And you've loved God and His Word more every day.
This has made all the difference.

I love you to infinity plus one!

CONTENTS

MY HOPE FOR YOU— BIG WAVE BIBLE CONFIDENCE

AS FORTY-FOOT WAVES SURGED into Waimea Bay on the North Shore of Oahu, forty surfers charged toward them.[1] The 2023 Eddie Aikau Big Wave Invitational drew surfers from around the world to ride what few dared.

These forty surfers were either insane or confident.

Assuming they're all of sound mind, how do big wave surfers gain the confidence to take on 40-foot walls of crushing water? The same way we become confident in surfing the heights and depths of the Bible. They ease into it. They wade in.

Big wave surfers first learn the basics: how waves react to the wind, reefs, and tides. The most effective methods to maneuver a bottom turn, cut back, and carve. The intricacies of longboards, shortboards, and eventually a gun surfboard.

In time, these men and women master barrels and popping up on the face of a towering wave with confidence and joy. Whatever intimidation they feel the first time they paddle out ultimately gives way to exhilaration as they discover the excitement of big wave surfing.

They're hooked.

As we ease into the Bible, we wade into the basics. How the 1,189 chapters and 66 books fit together to form one glorious, life-giving story. The most effective methods for reading and studying the Bible for transformation. The intricacies of the Bible's organization, genre, and translations.

In time, the Bible eventually masters those who trust in and follow Christ and fills us with confidence and joy. Whatever intimidation we feel the first time we open this massive book ultimately gives way to exhilaration as we discover more and more the greatness of our God and His Word.

We're hooked—and transformed.

STUDYING *EASE INTO THE BIBLE* WITH A GROUP

IF YOU'D LIKE TO study *Ease into the Bible* with a group, you can download a free Group Bible Study Guide on my website: JeanWilund.com.

Under the *Ease into the Bible* tab, you'll find group discussion questions and other resources to help you and your group get the most out of this book.

CHAPTER 1

THE BIBLE IS LIKE RHUBARB

THE BIBLE IS A bit like rhubarb. Until we understand it, we're not sure what to do with it.

Rhubarb is a reddish-pink, celery-type vegetable, but we don't treat it as a vegetable. We sweeten it to the level of fruit and serve it as a treat. It tastes uniquely delicious, if we can get past its fibers that look like someone stirred hair into our dessert or jam.

The first time I encountered rhubarb, my husband and his siblings were shoving each other aside to snag jars of their mom's bright-pink jam. I decided then that either rhubarb makes the best preserves, or I'd married into a strange family.

I took a cautious, but hopeful, bite.

Once I tasted and saw that rhubarb is everything they'd promised, I was changed. I became a rhubarb lover, hairs and all.

The Bible—Hairs and All

The Bible is a book, but we don't treat it like other books. For one thing, we don't know whether to read it from the beginning or jump around within its 1,189 chapters and 66 books.

It's full of stories, but it's not a novel. It tells the history of God's works and plans for humankind, but it's more than a history book.

It contains so many different literary genres, it may actually cover them all. Or at least most of them, including horror. (Ever read the book of Judges?)

The Bible sends the hearts of Christians into heights of rejoicing from Genesis to Revelation, but we could do without the icky parts—the hairy parts. (The laws about bodily fluids alone in Leviticus make my skin crawl.)

But once we taste and see that the Bible is not just good, it's the most glorious book ever written, we're changed. We become Bible lovers, hairs and all.

Taste and See

The Bible changes us, but not because it's the literary wonder that it is. We're changed because it's unique above all other books. It's the very Word of God. It's Christ's unfailing words of eternal life and the power of God to save and transform even the most unwilling heart.

Yet, until we taste and see for ourselves, the Bible sits on our shelf as if it were any other book.

My husband's college roommate never tasted his mom's rhubarb jam. While Larry feasted, his roommate missed out simply because he didn't like the way rhubarb looked. He refused to try it.

Despite the Bible being the best-selling book of all time, many hesitate to taste of it. We may display a Bible on our bookshelf with its gilded pages and decorative cover, but its vast size intimidates us. It's not a quick read. The ancient cultures and idioms confuse the casual reader. Some of the scary parts terrify us because they carry eternal significance.

But since you're reading this, I assume you're curious enough about the Bible that you're at least cautiously hopeful. Whether you just bought your first Bible, or you own a collection, my prayer is that this little book will instill you with confidence that you can taste and see that the Bible is far better than rhubarb—and any other book in history. That you will sit down each day with God's Word, eager for another taste until you've devoured it all, and find that you are changed.

> The instruction of the LORD is perfect,
> renewing one's life;
> the testimony of the LORD is trustworthy,
> making the inexperienced wise.
> The precepts of the LORD are right,
> making the heart glad;
> the command of the LORD is radiant,
> making the eyes light up.
> The fear of the LORD is pure,
> enduring forever;

the ordinances of the Lord are reliable
and altogether righteous.
They are more desirable than gold—
than an abundance of pure gold;
and sweeter than honey
dripping from a honeycomb.
In addition, your servant is warned by
them, and in keeping them there is
an abundant reward. (Ps. 19:7–11)

CHAPTER 2

THE OVERARCHING STORY (AND MAIN POINT) OF THE BIBLE

THE BIBLE IS ONE grand and true story.

All grand stories have a beginning, middle, and end. The beginning sets the stage and introduces the crisis. The middle raises the stakes and reveals how the hero ultimately saves the day. Happy endings bring the longed-for resolution and rest.

True stories with happy endings are the best.

So are true heroes.

Jesus is the greatest and truest hero. His unparalleled story is not a work of fiction or fantasy. It's historical (and future) fact. Christ's true story is the *gospel* told from Genesis to Revelation.

The Gospel Story

The original Greek word for *gospel* (*euangelion*) means "good news" or "good message." The gospel of Jesus Christ is the message of salvation, which makes the good news the best news because the bad news is devastating.

No matter how many times I read the Bible, my heart races during the bad news sections like it does when I read retellings of the *Titanic*. Maybe this time, the ship won't sink. Maybe this time, Adam and Eve won't plunge the world into sin. Maybe this time the crowd won't look at their Savior and shout, "Crucify Him!"

But the gospel story remains the same—shocking, gripping, and dire.

And glorious.

It's glorious because just as the beginning and middle never change, neither will the end. To understand the ending, though, we first need to understand the beginning.

The Beginning

Before the beginning of time, there's always been God. And nothing else. Only God the Father, God the Son, and God the Holy Spirit.

To help us understand what our finite minds can't fully grasp, scholars call this divine three-in-one being the *Trinity* (also sometimes called the *Godhead*). Three distinct Persons who share one divine and perfect nature.

From the first verse of the Bible, God introduced the truth of His triune nature by using the Hebrew plural word for God—*Elohim*.

> In the beginning God [Elohim] created
> the heavens and the earth. (Gen. 1:1)

In other words, the Father, Son, and Holy Spirit created the heavens and the earth together. But why? Given this triune nature of our God, it's a curious thing that the Trinity would want to create other beings at all. After all, since eternity past, the Father, Son, and Holy Spirit have existed together in perfect unity, holiness, and relational fullness. Perfect contentment and love. They've never experienced a need because they've never experienced a lack. They can't. Such is the nature of being perfect. Of being God.

Since the triune Godhead clearly didn't create us out of need, why then, were we created? For two exciting reasons:

First, our three-in-one God created us, not because He needs us, but because He wants us—even knowing everything we'd ever do, including bring sin into the world and cost Jesus His blood on the cross. God made us in His image and likeness—or more accurately, as God says in Genesis 1:26 when referring to His triune nature, "in *our* image"—all for His glory and pleasure.[1]

Second, we were created "for good works" (Eph. 2:10), or as Christ said, to produce "much fruit" (John 15:5). God created us to serve as rulers over the earth, guardians of His creation, and to multiply image-bearing worshippers across the earth (Gen. 1:26, 28).

As image-bearers (likenesses) of God, we're thinking, reasoning, and emotional beings with a will. On top of this, we're capable of being merciful, good, patient, and so on. These shared attributes of God give us the unique ability to know and worship Him and to reflect certain aspects of His nature to a watching world.

Unfortunately, because of the bad news, our expressions of God's perfect attributes are imperfect. While God can never change (He's immutable), we change by the second. ("I love you! I hate you!" "I'm so full, I can't eat another bite. Oh, look! Brownies.") Like God, we can offer grace, mercy, and forgiveness and experience love, joy, and peace, but in us, these are often fleeting.

Like liquid gold slipping through our fingers, we struggle to hold onto God's shared attributes. To faithfully feel and demonstrate them. But oh, how we can hold onto anger. God's wrath is always righteous anger over sin, whereas ours is frequently baseless tantrums.

Our sin and God's righteous anger bring us to the devastating conflict in the gospel story. To the crisis. To the bad news.

The Bad News

When God created the heavens and the earth, He also created angels and the first man and woman.[2] All good news until sin entered the picture.

Sin is anything that causes us to rebel against God and His commands. It's choosing our way and our rule over His.

As the Bible tells us, the sin of pride rose in one of the greatest angel's heart. The angel rebelled against God's rule and coerced many of the others to rebel with him. Their coup failed, and God cast them out of heaven.[3]

The Bible calls the leader of the fallen angels *Satan*, which means adversary.[4] He remains the adversary against all God loves and all who love God, beginning with Adam and Eve.

God placed Adam and Eve in the garden to rule over the earth. He gave them the fruit of every tree to eat—except the fruit from one tree. God said if they ate from the Tree of the Knowledge of Good and Evil, they would die. Not break out in a rash—die.[5]

Through this one "Thou shalt not" Satan found his weapon to destroy God's most loved creation. He disguised himself as a harmless serpent (I suppose serpents weren't scary yet!) and slinked up to Eve. While Adam looked on, Satan planted a thorny seed of doubt in her heart about God's Word and His character.

Satan lied.

He told Eve, "No! You will certainly not die. . . . God knows that when you eat it your eyes will be opened and you will be like God, knowing good and evil" (Gen. 3:4–5).

Although Adam and Eve lacked nothing, thoughts like, *Is God withholding good from us? Is God a liar?* sprouted in their hearts and spawned discontentment and pride.

We can rule ourselves.

We can determine what is good and what is evil.

We can be like God.

Eve gave into Satan's temptation of self-rule, rebelled against God, and ate the fruit He'd forbidden. Adam joined her.[6]

They traded God's benevolent rule for sin's tyranny. They exchanged friendship with God for submission to Satan.

While Satan had lied, he was right about one thing. Adam and Eve now knew both good (God) and evil (sin and Satan).[7]

Sin entered the world that day and as God promised, it brought death—instant spiritual death and eventual physical death—to them and their descendants.[8]

Their God-given nature twisted into a sin nature. Thoughts like, *I'll do it just this once. Come on, you know you want to,* and *That's not fair, God. You're ruining my life!* now ruined their hearts and infected their descendants.

Even today, we're all born spiritually dead, unable by our own power to throw off sin's rule. After all, dead people can't do anything. Without God's intervention, we can't escape sin's horrifying penalty of hell—a real place of eternal torment where all who reject Christ and His salvation experience God's wrath and are cut off from Him forever.[9]

The stakes couldn't be higher.

If God didn't intercede, all hope was lost for Adam and Eve—and for us.

(*Devastating* is too tame of a word to describe their helpless state.)

The good news is that, from before time began, God had already interceded.

(*Good* is too mild of a word to capture the fullness of relief and joy this news brings.)

In eternity past, God had already chosen our Savior—our true Hero.[10]

The Hero

With sin's introduction into the world, the dark backdrop was now laid—a backdrop against which God would display His glory (the sum of all His attributes).[11]

The deeper the darkness, the brighter the Truth shines—and the easier we can see the Light.

As Adam and Eve ate the fruit, Satan thought he'd destroyed them and frustrated God's plan, but no one can frustrate God's plan. No one. Since before the foundation of the world, (before there was even a need), God had already secured Adam and Eve's salvation—and the salvation of all who believe in Jesus—through the gospel.[12]

In the garden that day, God proclaimed the glorious gospel to Satan—while Adam and Eve listened:

> "I will put hostility between you and the
> woman, and between your offspring and
> her offspring. He will strike your head,
> and you will strike his heel." (Gen. 3:15)

Here in the first gospel declaration, God promised that although hostility would rise between Satan's offspring (all who hate God) and Eve's bloodline (which eventually leads to Jesus), a coming Hero would settle the hostility once and for all by defeating Satan and all the world-altering effects of his deception.

Satan would strike the Hero's heel. (Some interpret this as inciting men to crucify Jesus. Others interpret it as all the ways Satan tried to trip up Jesus in His gospel mission from the day of His birth to the day of His death.) The Hero, however, would prevail by crushing Satan's head. (Many interpret this as the Hero giving His life on the cross for sin and sealing Satan's eternal doom.)

The winner between the two is clear—after all, it is possible to recover after being struck on the heel, but no one can survive a crushed head.

The Middle

Everything that transpired in the beginning set the stage for the middle of Christ's gospel story and its chilling climax. The Old Testament records dramatic accounts God ordained to display the truths the world needed to know (and still needs to know). He wove into these thirty-nine Old Testament books more than three hundred prophecies about Jesus to prepare the way for His coming with salvation.

The New Testament records Jesus's fulfillment of every prophecy of His first coming including His crucifixion and resurrection from the dead. He proved He's the true Messiah—the Savior God promised in Genesis 3:15.

We can't grasp the complete picture of God's plan without both the Old and New Testaments. These sixty-six books bring the harsh truth to light that every human in history (including us) is a sinner who loves our sin and needs a Savior.

This is the wonder of the gospel story—the story of the Bible.

The Climax

Jesus came into the world in human flesh and lived among His creation. He fed, healed, and raised people from the dead. And He forgave their sins.

Then His own people crucified Him.

They murdered their Messiah and Savior.

Why?

Despite the numerous miracles Jesus performed, the Jewish leaders didn't believe He was the Messiah, the Son of God. They saw Jesus as a threat to their power.

The most insidious evil the world has ever known served as the black-velvet backdrop for the greatest rescue and expression of love the world has ever witnessed. On the cruel cross, the holiness, justice, and wrath of God met with His mercy, grace, and love in the sinless One—in Christ. Jesus paid the full penalty for sin on the cross so we don't have to. By His blood He redeemed us for Himself.

After He died, Jesus was buried in a sealed tomb and guarded by Roman soldiers. All hope seemed lost for His followers. But on the third day, Jesus rose to life and walked out of the grave. For the believer, His resurrection reversed the death-curse humanity has suffered under since Genesis 3. Jesus broke sin's power, crushed Satan's head, and destroyed death's sting.[13] Through His death and resurrection, Christ purchased the gift of eternal life for all who believe in Him.

> For the wages of sin is death, **but** the gift of
> God is eternal life in Christ Jesus our Lord.
> (Rom. 6:23, emphasis mine)

The Hinge of History

Everything in the Bible either points forward or backward to the cross. Christ's death, burial, and resurrection is the hinge of history that leads us to the glorious end.

Old Testament believers received salvation by looking forward in faith to Christ's coming.

New Testament believers (that's us) receive salvation by looking back in faith.

The repentant thief who hung next to Christ on the cross didn't have to look forward or backward. He looked straight into Jesus's eyes.

"Jesus," the thief said, "remember me when you come into your kingdom" (Luke 23:42).

Jesus responded to the thief's clear display of faith: "Truly I tell you, today you will be with me in paradise" (v. 43).

Jesus's resurrection flipped the gospel story's seeming trajectory from hopeless despair to unfathomable delight. He is alive forevermore! And so are all who believe in Him.

Forty days after Christ's resurrection, He rose back (ascended) into heaven where He sits and rules at the right hand of God until the time has come for the glorious end.[14]

The End

The end of the gospel story is the beginning of forever. Christ described it in vivid color in the book of Revelation.

It's the return of the King when Christ will gather His bride (the church) to Himself, and we'll receive our glorified bodies—our glory-hallelujah-sin-is-dead-forever bodies.

Christ will then judge all who have rejected Him; destroy sin, Satan, and death forever; and usher in His eternal kingdom—a more glorious kingdom than we can imagine.

The end of the gospel story promises the resolution and rest we yearn for now and forever—so long as we have truly believed in Christ. Only in Christ can we find our rest. This is why we need the beginning, middle, and end of the story. It's why we need the whole Bible.

This Is Our Story

Understanding the story of the Bible makes us realize we're not just reading the history of God's people, Christ's life, death, and resurrection, and the beginning of the church. We're reading our story.

We weren't slaves to a cruel Pharaoh in Egypt with Israel in Exodus, but we're slaves to sin today—and sin is the cruelest ruler.

We didn't stand at the foot of Mt. Sinai and promise God we'd obey His every command and then immediately worship a golden statue as if it were God. Nor were we sent into captivity in Assyria or Babylon with the Israelites. But like them, we choose our sin over God and His law as often as we think we can get away with it.

We didn't stand in the crowd before the Roman Governor Pilate as he asked the Jews what he should do with Jesus. We didn't shout, "Crucify Him!" but our sins sent our Savior to the cross as surely as their cries did.

We didn't watch Jesus rise into heaven and return to the Father, but we'll see Him return. And we'll all stand before His throne one day.

Every book in the Bible opens our eyes to the seriousness and destructiveness of sin and our desperate need for a Savior—for a true Hero.

Every chapter displays irrefutable evidence of who Christ is and who we are—and who we aren't (God).

Every verse propels us toward trusting God and believing in the gospel of Jesus Christ. His story is the grandest in history, and He is the truest Hero—and the main point of the Bible.

It's all about Him.

CHAPTER 3

UNDERSTANDING THE UNIQUENESS OF JESUS

THROUGHOUT JESUS'S LIFE ON earth, people called Him many things.

Much true: The Christ. The Messiah. God.

Much false: A liar. A blasphemer. A servant of Satan.

God proclaimed exactly who Jesus is: "This is my beloved Son, with whom I am well-pleased" (Matt. 3:17). On the Mount of Transfiguration, God told Peter, James, and John: "This is my beloved Son; listen to him!" (Mark 9:7).

From Genesis to Revelation, the Bible reveals:

Jesus

Christ

is the

uncreated and eternal

sinless Son of God.

The

visible

image

of our

invisible

God.

> For a child will be born for us, a son will
> be given to us, and the government will
> be on his shoulders. He will be named
> Wonderful Counselor, Mighty God,
> Eternal Father, Prince of Peace. (Isa. 9:6)

Jesus's name (*Iesous* in New Testament Greek) comes from His Hebrew name *Yeshua,* which means "The Lord is salvation." His title, Christ (*Christos* in Greek), comes from the Hebrew word for *Messiah,* which means Anointed One.

Whenever God called someone to serve as a king, prophet, or priest, he was anointed with oil to show God had set him apart for the Lord's service. From eternity past, God set His Son, Jesus the Messiah (the Christ), apart to serve as the perfect Prophet, Priest, and King.[1]

Jesus came as the perfect Prophet to proclaim the way to salvation, Priest to present Himself as the final sacrifice for sin, and King to rule with righteousness forever.

Only Jesus could serve as the final and perfect sacrifice because only a sinless person could pay the penalty for someone else—for us. Only Jesus was born without sin and lived a perfect life free of sin.

God couldn't simply overlook or forgive our sins without its payment being made. While ignoring our sin would satisfy God's mercy, it wouldn't satisfy His justice or wrath. He cannot be untrue to all of His nature.

The only possible way for us to be free of sin's payment was for our holy God to become man and take our place. Jesus, the second Person of the Trinity in human form (incarnate), is that divine Man. He left His throne in heaven and wrapped Himself in human flesh but without our sin. We're all born sinners. Jesus was not.

Jesus didn't inherit Mary's or Joseph's sinful spiritual DNA. He was conceived by the Holy Spirit in His mother, Mary, when she was a virgin. Joseph was not His father.

Even as Jesus grew up and lived in the world, He never sinned. Not once.

At the time God had planned from eternity past, Jesus's enemies nailed Him to a cross. There God placed all our sins onto His Son and poured out His full and just wrath for sin onto Christ. After Jesus had paid sin's full penalty, He gave up His life.

Jesus died and was buried.

On the third day, God raised Jesus to life, proving Jesus's death satisfied sin's debt for all who will believe in Him.

Satan and his demons (fallen angels) know Jesus is the Son of God, but they despise His rule and recoil at obeying Him. They shudder, but they must submit.[2]

One day, all creation will bow before Jesus. Including us.[3] The question is: Will we bow in grateful joy or—like the demons—in tormented submission?

Apart from Christ, we have no hope.

In Christ, we're forever saved.

All these truths become clearer as we read God's Word, which is the point of *Ease into the Bible*. To encourage us to read the Bible—the whole Bible—so we can know, believe in, and faithfully follow and serve Jesus for our good and His glory.

But these are written so that you may
believe that Jesus is the Messiah, the Son
of God, and that by believing you may
have life in his name. (John 20:31)

CHAPTER 4

WHY WE CAN TRUST THE BIBLE

THE BIBLE OPENS WITH God speaking the world into existence.

"Let there be light!"

The Bible ends with a new world that doesn't need the light of a lamp or even the sun. God's glory will fill His kingdom with His light.

Some may read these accounts and dismiss the Bible as a fairy tale, especially when they discover the Bible also includes a talking donkey, a virgin birth, and a man walking on water.

With such stories, how can we trust the Bible, much less submit ourselves to it as the authority over our lives? How can we know it's God's Word, not a product of the imaginations of men?

These reasonable questions have been answered in thick books. This small book will only touch on the abundance of evidence. We'll begin by considering biblical testimonies.

Biblical Testimonies

The Bible's Testimony

The Bible has much to say about itself, including that *every* word was inspired (given or breathed out) by God.[1] Not just the parts that start with, "God said," or "It is written." None of the Scriptures came from the mind of man, but from God.[2]

The Bible also testifies that it's faithful, trustworthy, and divine.[3] Every Word in the Bible is true.[4] It accomplishes everything God sends it out to do.[5] It never fails.[6]

We can trust God's Word today and forever because it cannot become outdated or irrelevant. It proclaims that it remains the words of eternal life forever.[7]

The Testimony of Christ

Throughout Jesus's three-year ministry on earth, He declared God's Word is truth and testified to the faithfulness of all the Scriptures, quoting the Old Testament often.[8] He explained how all the Scriptures (the Old Testament at that time) spoke of Him—including the many resurrection prophecies and types.[9]

A biblical *type* is a person, event, or object that foreshadows or symbolizes Christ and/or His work in the New Testament. For instance, Passover and the Passover Lamb are biblical types of Christ and His crucifixion (Exod. 12:1–29; 1 Cor. 5:7).

WHY WE CAN TRUST THE BIBLE

Jesus fulfilled every one of the more than three hundred Old Testament prophecies that spoke of His first coming. (He'll fulfill the rest when He returns.)

Without Jesus's miraculous resurrection, His claims of being God and the promised Messiah would've proven false. But Jesus did rise from the dead. More than five hundred eyewitnesses testified to seeing Him in the flesh, nail scars and all.

Testimonies from Outside the Bible

Multiple ancient records from outside the Bible confirm biblical accounts. Rather than quote testimonies of early church fathers who we'd expect to agree with the Bible, I'll note two significant non-Christian testimonies. These historians had no reason to corroborate New Testament claims if they didn't believe they were facts.

In AD 64, the Roman historian Tacitus recorded the account of Jesus's crucifixion:

> Therefore, to stop the rumor, Nero substituted as culprits and punished in the utmost refinements of cruelty, a class of men, loathed for their vices, whom the crowd styled Christians. Christus, the founder of the name, had undergone the death penalty in the reign of Tiberius, by sentence of the procurator Pontius Pilatus, and the pernicious superstition was checked for a moment, only to break out once more, not merely in Judea, the home of the disease, but in the

capital itself, where all things horrible or shameful in the world collect and find a vogue.[10]

Around AD 93–94, the Jewish historian Josephus wrote about Jesus many times, including the following selection:

> At this time there appeared Jesus, a wise man [if indeed one ought to refer to him as a man]. For he was a doer of startling deeds, a teacher of people who received the truth with pleasure. And he gained a following both among many Jews and among many of Greek origin. [He was the Messiah-Christ.] And when Pilate, because of an accusation made by the leading men among us, condemned him to the cross, those who had loved him previously did not cease to do so. [For on the third day he appeared to them again alive, just as the divine prophets had spoken about these and countless other marvelous things about him.] And up until this very day the tribe of Christians, named after him, has not died out. —*The Antiquities of the Jews* (18:63–64)[11]

Archeological Testimonies

The Dead Sea Scrolls

In 1947, a young Bedouin shepherd discovered one of the greatest archeological finds in history as he wandered near the Dead Sea in Israel in search of a lost goat. When he tossed a stone high into an opening in the cliffs, he heard clay jars crack. Inside the cliff, experts found more than nine hundred ancient documents in tightly sealed containers, where they'd rested for nearly two thousand years.

Archeologists, Jews, and Christians around the world celebrated the discovery of scrolls from every book of the Hebrew Bible (the Old Testament) except Esther. When experts compared these manuscripts to modern copies, the results stunned them.

Dr. W. F. Albright of Johns Hopkins University said, "My heartiest congratulations on the greatest manuscript discovery of modern times! . . . What an absolutely incredible find! And there can happily not be the slightest doubt in the world about the genuineness of the manuscript."[12]

Expert Gleason Archer said the scrolls "proved to be word for word identical with our standard Hebrew Bible in more than 95 percent of the text. The 5 percent of variations consisted chiefly of obvious slips of the pen and variations in spelling. They do not affect the message of revelation in the slightest."[13]

The Cairo Genizah

In 1896, a forgotten storehouse in Egypt shook the world of antiquities. *Genizahs* (storehouses) held unusable Hebrew documents containing God's name. For nearly a thousand years, the Cairo Genizah stored around ten thousand biblical documents dating from the fifth century, including the book of Ecclesiastes.[14]

How could ten thousand valuable ancient documents be forgotten? Sir Frederic George Kenyon, once a director of The British Museum, explains:

> The same extreme care which was devoted to the transcription of manuscripts is also at the bottom of the disappearance of the earlier copies. When a manuscript had been copied with the exactitude prescribed by the Talmud, and had been duly verified, it was accepted as authentic and regarded as being of equal value with any other copy. If all were equally correct, age gave no advantage to a manuscript; on the contrary, age was a positive disadvantage, since a manuscript was liable to become defaced or damaged in the lapse of time.[15]

Just as we don't transfer files onto a new computer and then carry both laptops around, the original biblical manuscripts weren't stored alongside their newer—and equally trusted—copies. Only God's *Word* is eternal—not the scrolls, parchments, or clay tablets. Not even the stone tablets God wrote on with His own finger in Exodus 31:18.

"The grass withers, the flowers
fade, but the word of our God
remains forever." (Isa. 40:8)

The Rosetta Stone

In 1799, Napoleon's soldiers dug up a boulder and helped crack the code of two ancient languages. The Rosetta Stone contains text in Greek and two unknown languages. With the Greek, scientists could now decipher both the hiero-glyphics and the local language of the ancient city of Rosetta. These languages confirmed biblical accounts.[16]

Behistun Rock

Archeologists verified more biblical accounts when they discovered an 82-foot-long ancient relief of King Darius I high on a cliff in modern-day western Iran. Its discovery enabled scholars to translate more Near Eastern languages and confirm more biblical accounts.[17]

26,000 New Testament Manuscripts

Original ancient manuscripts and copies are rare. This fact is why the presence of more than seventeen hundred cop-ies of Homer's *Iliad,* written in 800 BC astounds us. Far more amazing, however, is the approximately twenty-six thousand copies of portions of the New Testament.[18]

The New Testament is the most duplicated and preserved document in history. The flood of copies confirm that the Bible's recorded words and works have not been distorted from the original manuscripts.

Lawyer and professor John Warwick Montgomery wrote: "To express skepticism concerning the resultant text of the New Testament books . . . is to allow all of the classical antiquity to slip into obscurity, for no documents of the ancient period are as well-attested bibliographically as the New Testament."[19]

Are you still struggling, however, with how a talking donkey, a virgin birth, and a man walking on water can be true? Perhaps logical reasoning will help.

Logical Reasoning

Logic tells us we can trust every account in the Bible—including the impossible accounts—because an all-powerful God can turn impossibilities into historical events. The vast intricacies of creation demand an intelligent and powerful Creator. The evidence of creation and history points to the God of Genesis (the God of the Bible) as this Creator.

God spoke planets, stars, and living beings into existence. And He gave humans (as well as parrots, and a few dogs on YouTube) the ability to speak. It's reasonable to believe He can also make a donkey talk.

The God who created every body of water on the planet can certainly walk on it if He wants.

The God who created Adam out of dust and Eve from Adam's rib can easily orchestrate a virgin birth.

If the whole idea of God's existence seems strange to you, consider other ways people speak of a higher power. *Karma's going to get you. He got his mojo back. I don't believe in God, but I believe in a higher power.* These common phrases express a belief that in some way all human actions are being tracked by a higher power, evaluated morally, and then boomeranged back into the life of the human. Such abilities would require the higher power to have numerous abilities, including a perfect moral compass with which to judge all people fairly, total knowledge of the inner life and outer deeds of every person in every generation, and the power to make karma come back on them or restore their mojo. To recognize any higher force or power at work in this world is to believe in the supernatural—the miraculous.

> "Look, I am the LORD, the God over every
> creature. Is anything too difficult for me?"
> (Jer. 32:27)

If we say we believe in a higher power but doubt the Christian's God is the higher power, there's only one explanation—and it's the final stumbling block.

Faith: The Final Stumbling Block

Testimonies, physical evidence, and logical reasoning readily support the Bible's claims of truthfulness, but if you're still not convinced, dig deeper. The Bible stands up to all honest scrutiny. But even then, one stumbling block remains—faith.

Faith is a gift from God. Receiving the Holy Spirit (our Teacher) and the mind of Christ at salvation is also a gift.[20]

Only God's Spirit can reveal spiritual Truth and assure us of the Bible's infallibility and divine authority. "The natural person does not accept the things of the Spirit of God, for they are folly to him, and he is not able to understand them because they are spiritually discerned" (1 Cor. 2:14 ESV).

If you're a Christian and still struggle to understand the Bible, don't be discouraged. Christianity is a walk of faith. Keep reading and studying the Bible. As you seek Him through His Word, you'll come to understand and believe the One who indeed spoke through a talking donkey (Num. 22), came to earth through a virgin birth to save all who believe in Him from their sins (Matt. 1; Luke 1), and walked on water (Matt. 14).

> The revelation of your words brings
> light and gives understanding to
> the inexperienced. (Ps. 119:130)

CHAPTER 5
WHO WROTE THE BIBLE?

In the beginning God . . .
(Gen. 1:1)

THE BIBLE'S ULTIMATE AUTHOR is our perfect God, but He chose to write through imperfect men. The melting pot of biblical authors includes a Hebrew Egyptian prince who became a murderer, then a shepherd, and ultimately the leader of a wandering nation (Moses). The list of authors also includes a former hater of Christ and persecutor of Christians named Saul. After Jesus blinded Saul on a road, he embraced the truth of the gospel, began using his Roman name, Paul, and became one of the greatest Christian leaders in history. (Read his story in Acts 9.)

In perfect wisdom, God unfolded all we need to know over the course of more than fifteen hundred years using around forty different human authors. While these men may have failed royally at times (read about King David in 1 and 2 Samuel), they didn't fail in writing God's Word because the Holy Spirit directed them.

How Did the Holy Spirit Direct the Authors?

When Paul wrote: "All Scripture is inspired by God" (2 Tim. 3:16), the original Greek word he used for "inspired," (*theopneustos*) also means "God-breathed" or "God-spoken." God breathed out His Word through His authors.

But how?

Peter explained that the prophets were "carried along by the Holy Spirit," rather than by their own will (2 Pet. 1:20–21). King David said, "The Spirit of the LORD spoke through me, his word was on my tongue" (2 Sam. 23:2). God moved each of the Bible's authors in the same way, but this doesn't mean He turned them into robots. Each author used his own personality and writing style.

In ways only God fully knows, the Holy Spirit directed His exact message to a specific audience by His divine power. When the Bible proclaims it is incapable of being wrong about anything it teaches (inerrant), and that it cannot fail (infallible), God is talking about His *words*, not His human authors.

This doesn't mean, however, that we won't find certain characters uttering horrific lies in the Bible. After all, the Bible records the words of Satan, who is a liar and the father of lies (Gen. 3:5; John 8:44). Also, not every person in the Bible represented the truth or the Lord correctly. In the book of Job, for example, Job's three friends spouted many untruths about God, and God called them out. "He said to Eliphaz the Temanite, 'I am angry with you and your two friends, for you have not spoken the truth about me, as my servant Job has'" (Job 42:7).

Even though we can't trust what every human in the Bible said, we can trust that the Bible's inspired record of their words is accurate.

When Did the Authors Write?

More than twenty-nine authors wrote the thirty-nine Old Testament books between approximately 1400 BC to 400 BC.

Eight authors wrote the twenty-seven New Testament books between approximately AD 44 to AD 96.

In the period between both Testaments, God remained silent for four hundred years. During this time, He didn't raise up prophets to speak to His people or call anyone to write His words.

Then Jesus came.

After the church was instituted and Jesus returned to heaven, God called certain men to pick up their pens and styluses and write the New Testament. To write what God's people need to know while we wait for Christ's return.

Which Languages Did the Authors Use?

The Bible contains three languages: Hebrew, Greek, and Aramaic.

The Old Testament authors wrote mostly in Hebrew, the language of the nation of Israel, with a smattering of Aramaic in Daniel and Ezra (Dan. 2:4b–7:28; Ezra 4:8–6:18; 7:12–26).

Scholars aren't sure why the authors switched to Aramaic, except for when the passages quoted Aramaic documents.

The New Testament authors wrote predominately in ancient Greek, the common language of the Roman Empire, which ruled Israel at the time. (There are a few instances of Aramaic scattered throughout, but the vast majority is written in Greek.)

Ancient Writing Materials

In the book of Job, the author mentioned scrolls, lead, and stone along with an iron "stylus" (or "pen" in the ESV) (Job 19:23–24). Each Bible author used the writing tools of their day.

- **Scrolls:** Scrolls were typically made of leather or papyrus (a common plant of reeds glued together). The authors wrote on them with a "pen" dipped into ink.
- **Stone:** God wrote the Ten Commandments onto stone with His own finger. Twice. (Moses broke the first set. He had a good reason. See Exodus 32:1–19.) Every other author who wrote on stone needed a chisel.
- **Tablets:** God told Isaiah and Habakkuk to write on tablets (Isa. 30:8; Hab. 2:2–3). The tablets were most likely wood or clay, on which they carved using a stylus.

- **Parchment and Vellum:** Parchment and vellum were animal skins written on with pens dipped into ink (2 Tim. 4:13).

The Bible's Known Authors

Most, but not all, of the Bible's authors served as either a prophet (God's chosen spokesmen), a priest (God's servants in the temple), or an apostle (Christ's chosen leaders, called to establish the church). Two were kings (David and Solomon). Nehemiah was the cupbearer (personal servant) to a Babylonian king. Daniel served as a trusted advisor to three Babylonian kings (Nebuchadnezzar, Darius, Belshazzar).

Dr. Luke was the only Gentile author. James and Jude were Jesus's half brothers. (They shared the same mother, but not the same father. Jesus was conceived by the Holy Spirit.) Interestingly, neither James nor Jude believed in Jesus until after His resurrection, but they both became authors of the Bible and important leaders in the church.

The Bible's Anonymous Authors

Some of the Bible's authors remain a mystery. For whatever purpose, God didn't instruct each to sign his book or letter.

How can we trust what these authors wrote if we don't know who they are?

We can trust the anonymous authors today because the recipients of their messages knew and trusted them then.

Because their messages remained in alignment with the theological truths within the other books of the Bible, their audiences embraced their messages as being inspired by God and passed them down to us.

It's All about Christ

No matter which author God used or how much some of them failed in life, each faithfully wrote as God directed and pointed us to Christ. From Genesis to Revelation, it's all about Him.

> The grace of the Lord Jesus be with
> everyone. Amen. (Rev. 22:21)

CHAPTER 6

HOW GOD GAVE US THE SIXTY-SIX BOOKS OF THE BIBLE

GOD MOVED AND DIRECTED the authors of the Bible in what to write, but did He determine the selection of books to include in our Bible? Did God declare which books would be the *Canon of Scripture*—His final, holy, and authoritative Word? How did we get the Bible we have today?

The Canon of Scripture

Before the first author penned the first words in the Bible, God had already chosen which books would become the Holy Bible. Which would be the *canon*—or, as the original Greek word defines *canon,* the "measuring rod, rule, and standard" for the Holy Scriptures.

Just as stamping an artist's name on a painting doesn't make it authentic, stamping God's name onto an ancient text doesn't make it God's authoritative Word. For the people of God to submit themselves to a book's commands and

teachings, it had to bear its Creator's unique "fingerprints"—
His obvious traits. It's important for us to understand that the
canon of Scripture we have today (the sixty-six books of our
Bible) weren't *chosen*. Each book was *recognized* as displaying
the obvious traits of the Author—God.

The Old Testament Canon

The ancient Jewish leaders recognized and accepted the
thirty-nine books we have in our modern Old Testament as
God's inspired and authoritative Word. After the prophet
Malachi wrote his book, God closed the canon of the Old
Testament Scriptures with four hundred years of silence.

When Jesus came to earth, He affirmed the Old
Testament canon. He quoted from it often and declared: "the
Scripture cannot be broken" (John 10:35). In other words,
God's Word cannot be invalidated or contradicted.

Before the cross, Jesus said the Scriptures "testify about
me" (John 5:39). After His resurrection, He explained where
and how the Scripture speaks of Him to two men as the three
walked together: "Then beginning with Moses and all the
Prophets, he [Jesus] interpreted for them the things concerning himself in all the Scriptures" (Luke 24:27).

The New Testament Canon

The early church councils didn't give us the New
Testament. They recognized what God had given us.
Theologian J. I. Packer wrote: "The church no more gave us

the New Testament canon than Sir Isaac Newton gave us the force of gravity. God gave us gravity, by his work of creation, and similarly he gave us the New Testament canon, by inspiring the individual books that make it up."[1]

When God inspired the books of the New Testament, the church leaders circulated their books among the other churches. It was clear to them which books were inspired—which ones displayed the breath of God.

Over time, as the apostles began to die, the New Testament church leaders knew they needed to preserve their teachings (1 Cor. 11:2; 2 Thess. 2:15). The apostolic fathers (a well-known group of early church leaders) quoted most of the epistles in our Bible as inspired.

Sometime in the mid-fourth century, Athanasius of Alexandria, Egypt, wrote a letter confirming the same twenty-seven books of our New Testament. His letter stated that he had "decided to set forth in order the writings that have been put in the canon, that have been handed down and confirmed as divine."[2] He didn't choose the books. He recognized that which was already accepted as originating from God.

In AD 393, the Council of Hippo recognized the same twenty-seven New Testament books as did a council of church leaders who met in Carthage, Africa, in AD 397. They, too, recognized the same twenty-seven books in our modern Protestant Bible.[3]

What Qualified a Book to Be Recognized as Scripture?

Church leaders recognized and affirmed the canon of Scripture by holding to certain overriding principles. If a book didn't meet *all* their criteria, such as the ones below, the book was rejected as inspired.

1. Did one of God's prophets, apostles, or another widely accepted spokesman of God write the book?
2. Is the book historically accurate and in no way contradicts what God has revealed in already-accepted Scripture?
3. Did the overall church body receive the book as God's inspired Word and affirm its authority over their lives by submitting themselves to the book's teachings?[4]

The Apocrypha

The Catholic and Eastern Orthodox Bibles include extra books known as the *Apocrypha* or *Deuterocanonical*. These books were written before the New Testament and were never accepted into the ancient canon of Hebrew Scriptures (the Old Testament). The early church rejected them as well because Jesus never quoted from these books and some thinkers hold that their teachings contradict accepted Scripture.[5]

Christ Closed the Canon

Just as Malachi and the four hundred years of silence closed the Old Testament canon, the book of Revelation and Christ's ensuing silence closed the New Testament canon.

All Scripture is now closed.

When God is silent, we should be too. We never want to put words into God's mouth—or into His Word. (Neither do we want to take His words out.)[6]

God has given us everything we need to know until Christ returns (Rev. 22:18–19).

The Bible doesn't tell us everything we *want* to know ("When exactly will Christ return? Which job should I take?"), but it tells us everything we *need* to know.

The sixty-six books of God's inspired Word are sufficient to meet the spiritual needs of every heart through Jesus Christ our Lord.

> All Scripture is inspired by God
> and is profitable for teaching, for
> rebuking, for correcting, for training
> in righteousness, so that the man of
> God may be complete, equipped for
> every good work. (2 Tim. 3:16–17)

CHAPTER 7

UNDERSTANDING HOW THE BIBLE IS ORGANIZED

IF I HANDED YOU a book, where would you start reading? What if I handed you a Bible?

> The Bible is a book of sixty-six books split into two divisions—two Testaments.[1]
>
> The first division—the Old Testament—has thirty-nine books.
>
> The second division—the New Testament— has twenty-seven books.

Again, where would you start reading? In the Old Testament? The New Testament? Why do we even have two testaments? And what is a testament?

Two Testaments—One Story

The word *testament* comes from Hebrew and Greek words that mean "binding together, covenant, promise, or agreement."

The Bible is one story of God fulfilling His irrevocable gospel promise with His children through Christ. He explained and unfolded this story in two stages of history—the Old Testament (before Christ came in flesh) and the New Testament (after Christ came in flesh).

The Old Testament

The thirty-nine books of the Old Testament cover the period between Creation and the end of the era of prophets (around 440 BC).[2]

God opened the Old Testament at Creation, when He formed Adam and Eve in paradise, where everything was good—very good (Gen. 1:31).

He closed the Old Testament with a promise that points to Christ because the world had become bad—very bad (Mal. 4:4–6).

In between the times, God recorded the riveting history of His works in the world and Israel, the nation He created to know Him and prepare the world for Christ's coming salvation. God displayed His faithfulness and gave us *types* (shadows/illustrations) and glimpses of Jesus, who was always present—though His people rarely realized it.

Tucked into the pages of the Old Testament, God had concealed a mystery He didn't fully reveal until the New Testament. The ancient theologian St. Augustine said it well: "In the Old Testament the New is concealed, in the New the Old is revealed."[3]

The marvelous mystery hidden in the Old Testament is the church—people belonging to God from *every* tribe and nation of the world, not just the nation of Israel. Believers who have confessed Jesus as Messiah and Lord.[4]

Between the Testaments

Four hundred years of silence followed the Old Testament during which God gave no new messages to His people. Malachi was the last prophet of God until the New Testament prophet John the Baptist.

During these four hundred years, God silently worked and only spoke through the testimony of creation and the Old Testament Scriptures.

The New Testament

The twenty-seven books of the New Testament open immediately before Christ's birth when He came as a baby, the Messiah and rightful King, born in obscurity in a humble stable. God closed the New Testament with Christ's glorious return and the coming of His eternal kingdom—the new heavens and earth—where He'll reign with all who love Him. In between these historic and glorious events, we witness the crucifixion and resurrection of Christ and the founding and growth of His church.

The (Surprising) Order of the Bible: Literary Genre

As important as history and the gospel message are, the Bible isn't organized around these truths. It's ordered by the main literary genre in each book. Knowing the Bible's genres may seem dull, but they help us interpret Scripture correctly since the genres guide our interpretation. We'll glance at genre as we consider the five main divisions of the Bible.[5]

Five Divisions of The Old Testament

1. The Pentateuch

Genesis, Exodus, Leviticus, Numbers, Deuteronomy

Moses wrote the first five books of the Bible called the *Pentateuch* ("five books"). They're also known as the *Law of Moses* and the *Torah*, which means "law" in Hebrew. The primary genre in these five books is *narrative*. Within the narrative, we see the subgenres: *law, history,* and *genealogy.*

Law uses legal language to express God's will and commands. God's giving Israel His law is one of the most pivotal (and enlightening) moments in history. God's law serves as both a mirror and a window. As a window, it allows us to see into God's character, nature, and ways. As a mirror, it shows us the reality of our reflection of Christ—and how little we truly reflect Him.

The New Testament reveals that God never designed His law to make men worthy of heaven, but to show us our utter unworthiness and our inability to live righteously before a holy God. "The law, then, was our guardian until Christ, so that we could be justified by faith" (Gal. 3:24).

History uses narrative to tell the story of actual events. In historical narrative, the author says what he means and means what he says.

Moses used historical narrative to record God's powerful works so we can know and trust in Him. These records are also examples for us to follow—or *not* follow, as in the case of Joseph's brothers. They threw him into a pit and sold him to slave traders (Gen. 37:12–36). (Don't sell your siblings. Be like Joseph, and trust God.)

Genealogy documents family lineages. God used genealogy to ensure Israel (and we) could trace Jesus through Mary and Joseph to David, Judah, Abraham, and Adam and Eve.

2. History

Joshua, Judges, Ruth, 1 and 2 Samuel, 1 and 2 Kings, 1 and 2 Chronicles, Ezra, Nehemiah, Esther

These twelve books mostly use the narrative genre to report the storied history of Israel. They chronicle the rise and fall of its kings, particularly David, and a few nasty queens. (Ever heard of Jezebel? Not a nice lady.)

They expose the depth of depravity when we ignore God's law and do what is right in our own eyes. Even God's people will sink to unimaginable evil when they chase after any other god than the One true God. Over and through every recorded event, we see God's holy hand prepare us for

Jesus through His displays of His sovereign power and long-suffering patience, mercy, and grace.

3. Wisdom and Poetry

Job, Psalms, Proverbs, Ecclesiastes, Song of Solomon

In the wisdom and poetry books, the authors often use clever sayings and poetic devices such as figurative language, symbolism, and parallelism (repeated words, phrases, or ideas to emphasize the same or opposite meaning). The authors used whichever devices best conveyed what God wants us to understand about Himself, ourselves, sin, Satan, and the world.

When interpreting wisdom and poetry books, it's best to look for the underlying meaning and authoritative truths the author is expressing by means of these literary devices. In Psalm 105, the psalmist uses powerful (and literal) narrative to declare God's mighty works among His people. In Psalm 23, King David uses metaphors to teach us the Lord is good to His people like a faithful Shepherd who leads His beloved flock and a generous Host who cares for His guests.

4. Major Prophets

Isaiah, Jeremiah, Lamentations, Ezekiel, Daniel

The five major books of the prophets are called "major" because of their major length—except Lamentations. (It only has five chapters.) Since the prophet Jeremiah wrote both Jeremiah (with its fifty-two chapters) and Lamentations, they're placed together in the Old Testament.

Prophets were special spokesmen of God who either *foretold* (proclaimed the future works of God) or *forthtold* (proclaimed the Word of God). Being a prophet was serious business. They watched over the hearts of God's people and gave encouragement and/or warnings as God directed them. They spoke as God commanded, even when they didn't understand the prophecies they announced. If they spoke anything that was not of God, but from their own heart, their words were lies, and they were to be put to death.[6]

God's prophets reminded His people of His faithfulness and promises, but they also delivered unpopular messages of coming judgment. Most of the prophets (major and minor) were ignored and persecuted. Many were killed. But they honored God and received eternal rewards beyond any momentary rewards they could have enjoyed on earth.

Keep in mind that while the prophetic books are their own genre, they often employ many literary devices we've seen before like metaphor, simile, poetry, etc., in order to advise, encourage, warn, and correct God's people. (For example, in Isaiah 64:8, the prophet Isaiah uses metaphor by calling God a potter and referring to humans as clay. As we know from Christ's words in John 4:24, God is Spirit— meaning, He does not have a body with which to sit on a literal stool as He fashions pots on a throwing wheel. But the corrective truth gleaned from the prophet Isaiah when we feel like we're the authority over our own lives is that *God* is our Creator, and therefore has total authority over His creation.)

5. Minor Prophets

Hosea, Joel, Amos, Obadiah, Jonah, Micah, Nahum, Habakkuk, Zephaniah, Haggai, Zechariah, Malachi

The twelve minor prophets wrote small books with massive messages. They warned, encouraged, convicted, and inspired God's people. They pointed to the coming of their Messiah and wrote of coming judgment on earth and at the end of time. Like the major prophets, they faced cruel treatment by those who hated their message.

Five Divisions of the New Testament

The New Testament shines a spotlight onto the works, promises, and teachings of Christ. They show us the way to salvation and what it looks like to live for Christ while we wait for His return.

1. The Gospels

Matthew, Mark, Luke, John

The uppercase word *Gospel* refers to the four books which proclaim the lowercase *gospel*—the good news of salvation in Christ. Each Gospel is named after the person the church in their day widely accepted as its author. Each wrote to a specific audience, whether Jews, Romans, Greeks, or Gentiles using various genre such as historical narrative, parables (fictional stories Jesus told to teach a specific truth), and discourse (Jesus's teachings/sermons).

The Gospels documented parts of Jesus's life, but the authors' goal wasn't to write Jesus's biography, but rather their testimony of Christ: "But these are written so that you may believe that Jesus is the Messiah, the Son of God, and that by believing you may have life in his name" (John 20:31).

2. History

Acts

The Acts of the Apostles uses narrative to record the history of the earliest years of the church. God established and built His church by the power of the Holy Spirit at work in and through the actions of the first century apostles.

3. The Pauline Epistles

Romans, 1 and 2 Corinthians, Galatians, Ephesians, Philippians, Colossians, 1 and 2 Thessalonians, 1 and 2 Timothy, Titus, Philemon

The word *epistles* comes from the Greek word *epistolē*, meaning "letter, message, or dispatch."[7] Biblical epistles were instructive letters designed to help the readers (Christians) understand Christianity's essential doctrines and to address specific challenges the churches and/or individuals faced.

The apostle Paul wrote thirteen epistles to specific churches or individuals. Most of the Pauline epistles followed the customary Greek structure similar to our modern letters. They opened with a greeting followed by the body of the message and ended with a salutation. Paul typically presented theological teaching followed by application (what it looks like to properly respond to the biblical teaching).

4. The General Epistles

Hebrews, James, 1 and 2 Peter, 1, 2, and 3 John, Jude

The general epistles were addressed to the church in general (Christians) rather than to a specific local church or individual, and focused on universal and foundational biblical truths. James, John, Peter, and Jude wrote seven of the general epistles. No one knows for sure which author wrote the book of Hebrews. The recipients knew, but they didn't leave a record.

5. Prophecy

Revelation

The last book in the Bible is the final revelation of Jesus Christ given to His disciple John. The official title is The Book of the Revelation to John, but most call it Revelation (except for those who mistakenly tack on an "s" and call it Revelations).

John wrote the book of Revelation as an *epistle* and *prophecy* from Jesus to seven specific churches in their day—and also to every church (and Christian) until Christ returns.

Revelation is well-known for John's use of *prophecy* with *apocalyptic* elements such as vivid symbolism and imagery that foretells coming disaster. (See the four beasts in Revelation 11:7; 13:1–18.)

Jesus commanded John to "write what you have seen, what is, and what will take place after this."[8] To accomplish His command, John wrote in a *narrative* style whenever the literal sense made sense, such as in the first nine verses in Revelation 1. When he couldn't properly describe in literal terms what he saw or heard, he used symbolism. In Revelation 1:14, John described Jesus using metaphors and similes: "The hair of his head was white *as wool*—white *as snow*—and his eyes *like a fiery flame*" (emphasis mine).

Revelation—and the Bible—ends with excited anticipation as we wait for Christ's glorious return.

> He who testifies about these things says,
> "Yes, I am coming soon." Amen! Come,
> Lord Jesus! The grace of the Lord Jesus be
> with everyone. Amen. (Rev. 22:20–21)

CHAPTER 8

THE CHRONOLOGICAL ORDER OF THE BIBLE

THE BIBLE HAPPENED IN real time in real history. But, as we saw in the last chapter, the Bible isn't organized based on its historical time line. If you ever tried to read straight through the Bible, you likely discovered this after Judges.

A true chronological reading of the Bible is complicated. It's hard to place a modern date on ancient history. The Bible writers kept time differently than we do. We mark time based on Christ's birth. This wasn't possible for the Old Testament writers, and it didn't become the standard until several hundred years after the Bible was compiled.

The Bible's authors tended to record time in relation to events such as the birth of a child or the reign or death of a king.

"Adam was 130 years old when he fathered a son" (Gen. 5:3).

"In the year that King Uzziah died" (Isa. 6:1).

"During the month of Nisan in the twentieth year of King Artaxerxes" (Neh. 2:1).

A true chronological reading also forces us to leap back and forth at times within different books because many books overlap.

After Israel settled in the Promised Land, God sent multiple prophets to address Israel's numerous sins. The prophets often wrote at the same time.

Psalms was written across many periods of Israel's history.

Kings and Chronicles were written at different times to different audiences, but they record much of the same history.

The four Gospels cover the life of Christ, but not always in chronological order.

Scholars have researched and analyzed the books to determine, to the best of their ability, the Bible's chronological order. To read the Bible in a more exact historical order, I recommend a chronological Bible such as the *CSB Day-by-Day Chronological Bible* or a chronological reading plan such as BlueLetterBible.org's free online plan.[1] [See chapter 9, "The Best (and Worst) Bible Reading Plans."] I've listed the Bible books on the next pages in the most basic historical order without accounting for the extensive overlapping of books. This list is based, not on when the books were written, but on when the biblical events took place in history, following a simplified order from the *CSB Day-by-Day Chronological Bible*.

The Most Basic Chronological Order of the Books of the Bible

Old Testament
1. Genesis
2. Job
3. Exodus
4. Leviticus
5. Numbers
6. Deuteronomy
7. Joshua
8. Judges
9. Ruth
10. 1 Samuel
11. 2 Samuel
12. 1 Chronicles
13. Psalms
14. 1 Kings
15. Song of Songs
16. Proverbs
17. Ecclesiastes
18. 2 Chronicles
19. 2 Kings
20. Jonah
21. Amos
22. Hosea
23. Isaiah
24. Micah
25. Nahum
26. Zephaniah
27. Habakkuk
28. Joel
29. Jeremiah
30. Obadiah
31. Lamentations
32. Ezekiel
33. Daniel
34. Ezra
35. Haggai
36. Zechariah
37. Esther
38. Malachi
39. Nehemiah

400 Years of Silence

New Testament
40. John
41. Matthew
42. Luke
43. Mark
44. Acts
45. James
46. Galatians
47. 1 Thessalonians
48. 2 Thessalonians
49. 1 Corinthians
50. 2 Corinthians
51. Romans
52. Philippians
53. Philemon
54. Colossians
55. Ephesians
56. Titus
57. 1 Timothy
58. 1 Peter
59. Hebrews
60. 2 Timothy
61. 2 Peter
62. Jude
63. 1 John
64. 2 John
65. 3 John
66. Revelation

CHAPTER 9

THE BEST (AND WORST) BIBLE READING PLANS

WHICH IS MORE IMPORTANT—READING the Bible or studying the Bible?

Neither. Neither is more important because both are vital.

When we read the Bible, we take it in like we would a letter or novel. We let the author speak to us, the words wash over us, and the whole message sink into our soul.

When we study the Bible, we dig into it like we would a treasure hunt. Not everything of value sits in plain sight. Some of its greatest treasures wait for those willing to dig to find it.

In this chapter, we'll look at the first step toward mining the immeasurable treasures in God's Word—reading the Bible.

The whole Bible.

I make this distinction because it took me around twenty-five years to realize that reading parts of the Bible isn't the same as reading the whole Bible. And it doesn't produce the same results.

Reading the Whole Bible

Before I first read the Bible from cover to cover, I hung out in the New Testament since I wanted to read about Jesus. (I didn't know He was also in the Old Testament.)

As much as I felt love for Jesus, I didn't read my Bible out of true desire, but out of duty. Good Christians read their Bible, right? I attended a growing church and lived in a close Christian community. My heart soared when I thought about God, but my emotions, fears, and sin still ruled me more than the Truth ruled me.

I couldn't keep the Greatest Commandment. I didn't love the Lord my God with all of my heart, soul, mind, and strength (Mark 12:30). I loved Him until loving Him interfered with my dreams and goals.

This had to stop.

In desperation, I turned to the Bible—the whole Bible. Surely the answer was in there somewhere on a page I'd never read or simply skimmed over.

But how does one read the whole Bible?

I decided I'd read it like any other book. I started on page 1 and read straight through to the end.

Reading the whole Bible changed my life. I'd barely begun reading Deuteronomy when I realized God was transforming my heart and mind. Long before I reached the last page of Revelation, I knew I'd read the entire Bible for the rest of my life. But I've never again wanted to read it straight through from Genesis to Revelation—for two reasons.

First, it took me ages to get to the New Testament.

Second, it took me ages to get back to the Old Testament.

As I read the Old Testament, I fell in love with it, but I missed the New Testament. As I read the New Testament, I missed my new friend, the Old Testament. Since then, I've used Bible reading plans that allow me to read each day from both Testaments.

What I haven't changed in my reading, however, are four commitments. I made two of the commitments before I started reading the whole Bible. I developed the other two by the time I finished. And I've never been the same.

Four Bible Reading Commitments

1. Read the Bible daily.

Since I was desperate for an immediate change, and the Bible is extraordinarily long, I knew anything less than a daily commitment wouldn't be enough. I woke up before everyone else, read my Bible, and prayed. I didn't read out of duty. I read out of desperation.

A passion for God's Word unexpectedly grew out of my daily habit. Before long, I was hooked. Each morning, I couldn't wait to read my Bible because of how it was changing my heart and mind—and I wasn't trying to change.

I've continued this daily commitment ever since. I had tasted the sweetness of God's Word, and it satisfied my soul. I work my schedule around reading the Bible, not the other way around, but I'm not a slave to my reading.

No matter what time of day we choose to read, time in God's Word should be a nonnegotiable part of our day, but we shouldn't stress when we miss. We're not earning points or a merit badge. We're getting to know the Lord and building our relationship with the God of the Universe—our Creator. We're sitting at our Savior's feet like Mary. (Read Luke 10:38–42 to find out what this means.)

> Like newborn infants, desire the pure milk
> of the word, so that by it you may grow
> up into your salvation, if you have tasted
> that the Lord is good. (1 Pet. 2:2–3)

2. Look for God on every page.

Once I decided to read the whole Bible, I opened to the first page and cried out to God, "I just want to know You! Show me You on every page."

I looked for what God revealed in each passage about His character, nature, and ways. What I saw stunned me. On each page of the Bible, I discovered a God I thought I knew but is greater than I could imagine. And I saw Jesus. On every page. Not just in the New Testament.

I discovered a transformational truth I'd never understood before: we'll never truly know and love the God of the Word apart from the Word of God.

The Bible is the primary way the Holy Spirit transforms our hearts and minds today because His Word is the primary way we can know God and Jesus Christ, our Lord.

Peter said it better:

> May grace and peace be multiplied to
> you **through the knowledge of God and
> of Jesus our Lord.** His divine power has

given us everything required for life and
godliness **through the knowledge of
him** who called us by his own glory and
goodness. (2 Pet. 1:2–3, emphasis mine)

3. Don't seek to master the Bible. Seek to let the Bible master you.

The Pharisees in Jesus's day had mastered the Scriptures,
but they refused to let the Scriptures master them. Over
time, the more I read and grew to know God better, the
more I realized God's Word was conquering my emotions,
my fears, and my sin. It was mastering me. I was beginning
to love what God loves and hate what God hates. I was being
sanctified—made more like Christ (Rom. 8:29).

The right goal for reading the Bible isn't to accumulate
knowledge or to learn how to improve ourselves. Knowledge
for knowledge's sake makes us prideful, and prideful people
are insufferable. Only God can shape and mold us into shining reflections of Christ. The best goal, the right goal, for
Bible reading and study is to know God and let His Word do
its perfect work in our hearts and minds.

For the word of God is living and
effective and sharper than any double-
edged sword, penetrating as far as the
separation of soul and spirit, joints and
marrow. It is able to judge the thoughts
and intentions of the heart. (Heb. 4:12)

4. Read the whole Bible for the rest of your life.

Long before I finished the Old Testament, I knew I'd continue to read the whole Bible for the rest of my life. To quote pastor and author A. W. Tozer, "It takes a whole Bible to make a whole Christian."[1] To quote my mom, "You'll never understand the New Testament until you understand the Old."

They're both right. Trust me. Strike that—trust God's Word. Read the whole Bible for the rest of your life.

> All Scripture is inspired by God
> and is profitable for teaching, for
> rebuking, for correcting, for training
> in righteousness, so that the man of
> God may be complete, equipped for
> every good work. (2 Tim. 3:16–17)

The Best (and Worst) Bible Reading Plans

The Worst Plan: No Plan

The worst reading plan is no plan. *Those who fail to plan, plan to fail* remains a popular saying for a reason. Without a plan, countless demands on our time will squeeze out our daily Bible reading.

We'll mean well, but we won't read the Bible until we either make a plan and stick to it, or we love the Bible so much we squeeze out other things for time to read it. This is why we need a plan.

It's hard to fall in love with a book we haven't fully read. But once we read the whole Bible with the right goal—to know God the Father, Son, and Holy Spirit—an undying love for God's Word can grow.

Worst Plan Runner-Up: A Verse a Day

We all experience days when reading one verse is a victory, but it should never be our plan. If my internet search is correct (the internet is always correct, right?) there are 31,102 verses in the Bible. This means, if we read one verse a day, it will take us more than eighty-five years to finish the Bible. Forget about remembering what you read those first seventy years.

Even the busiest person has time to read the Bible. How do I know? God never commands us to do something He won't empower us to do. He might, however, call us to be creative and/or give up something in our schedule.

God created time. He provides enough to read His Word. Let's take the time He provides. (Let's also not beat ourselves up when all we can manage at times is one verse. Christians are slaves of Christ, not our Bible reading plan.)

The Best Plan: The Whole Bible

The best reading plan is any plan that gets us into the whole Bible so the whole Bible gets into us.

My favorite Bible reading plans are those that help us see how beautifully God connected the whole Bible. One of my favorites is the *Robert Murray M'Cheyne Bible Reading Plan*.[2] The Bible makes even more sense as we see the overarching story develop to its climax and ultimate fulfillment. As we see our part in the story of Christ.

The Gospel Story Overview Plan

All sixty-six books reveal aspects of the gospel story. To read a shortened overview of the gospel in the Bible, Dr. R. C. Sproul recommended in his book *Knowing Scripture* to read the following twenty-five books in this order:

> Genesis, Exodus, Joshua, Judges, 1 and 2 Samuel, 1 and 2 Kings, Ezra, Nehemiah, Amos, Hosea, Jeremiah, Ecclesiastes, Song of Solomon, Psalms, Proverbs, Luke, Acts, Ephesians, 1 Corinthians, 1 Peter, 1 Timothy, Hebrews, and Romans.[3]

After you've read these books, either read the remaining books of the Bible or jump over to a whole Bible reading plan.

Never Give Up

The only way we fail in Bible reading is to quit. Never give up. No matter how long it takes.

Expect life to get in the way. Never give up.

Expect not to love every passage of the Bible. Never give up.

Seek to know God on every page. Let His Word do its work in your heart. And never give up.

To know God through the Bible—the whole Bible—is a priceless treasure worth any cost.

And you [Timothy] know that from
infancy you have known the sacred
Scriptures, which are able to give you
wisdom for salvation through faith
in Christ Jesus. (2 Tim. 3:15)

CHAPTER 10

WHICH BIBLE TRANSLATION IS BEST FOR ME?

I ONCE HEARD A speaker say we should only read the original Bible. The King James Bible.

I was so confused.

English wasn't a language when the Old and New Testament were written. The King James is not the original. But I agree we should read a Bible as close to the original manuscripts as possible—as long as we can understand it.

Do you understand Greek or Hebrew?

If not, thank the next Bible translator you meet for his or her part in providing us with a wealth of translations of God's Word.

Which is the best translation for us?

Does it even matter which translation we read as long as we're reading a Bible?

Actually, translations matter a great deal because not every Bible on the market is a faithful representation of God's inspired Word.

Understanding the translation process helps us make easier—and wiser—choices.

Bible Translation Methods

Faithful translators make it their goal to remain as true to the original text as possible while still making the Bible understandable for readers. It's not easy. Translation teams must properly decipher the original—and complex—grammar, sentence structures, idioms, genre, etc. If they do their work poorly, it can lead to Bibles which say things God's originally inspired Word never said.

Since translating the Bible properly is complicated, the most faithful Bible translations come from teams of qualified translators and editors working together rather than individuals working alone. The process begins with the original Hebrew, Aramaic, or Greek Scriptures and an *interlinear*.

Interlinear

An interlinear is a list of the original words in their original sentence order with the translated words in line above or below them. While the translated words may be an accurate translation, the sentences can be nearly incomprehensible.

Consider the following interlinear translation of Matthew 1:18.

> "Now of Jesus Christ the birth as follows was
> had been betrothed mother when His Mary
> to Joseph before came together they she was

found with child to be by Spirit the Holy."[1]
(Matt. 1:18 Interlinear BlueLetterBible)

Clearly more work needs to be done to transform this jumble of words into a coherent sentence that doesn't compromise the author's original meaning. Translators use one of four methods.

Word-for-Word: The Formal Equivalence Method

Translator's Goal: Remain as close as possible to the original wording and sentence structure to help maintain the author's original intent without sacrificing ease of understanding for the reader.

Reader Benefits: The formal equivalence method tends to be the most faithful to the original text because the translators simply say what the author said in an understandable way. As much as possible, they translate the text word for word. They don't interpret the author's meaning. These translations make great choices for Bible study.

Reader Challenges: Sometimes the wording sounds awkward, and the use of ancient phrases and idioms as well as unfamiliar culture references can make the passage's meaning hard to understand.

Matthew 1:18 Formal Equivalence Example: "Now the birth of Jesus the Messiah was as follows: when His mother Mary had been betrothed to Joseph, before they came together she was found to be pregnant by the Holy Spirit" (Matt. 1:18 NASB).

Popular Formal Equivalence Translations: New American Standard Bible (NASB), Legacy Standard Bible (LSB), Amplified Bible (AMP), English Standard Version (ESV), Revised Standard Version (RSV), King James Version (KJV), and New King James Version (NKJV).

Thought-for-Thought: Dynamic Equivalence Method

Translator's Goal: Convey the author's original meaning of the verse. While translators don't ignore the author's original sentence structure, they readily move words around to help clarify the meaning. Rather than word-for-word, this method seeks to match the author thought for thought. (This method is also known as the *functional equivalence method*.)

Reader Benefits: The dynamic equivalence method tends to result in a more readable and understandable text while remaining as faithful as possible to the original inspired manuscript. These can be a good choice for those new to the Bible.

Reader Challenges: When translators use this method, they must do a certain amount of interpreting of the passage's meaning. No matter how sincere the translators' efforts may be, they can misinterpret. Also, sometimes the original authors chose words for their dual meanings. This method runs the risk of inadvertently losing those dual meanings.

Matthew 1:18 Dynamic Equivalence Example: "This is how the birth of Jesus the Messiah came about: His mother Mary was pledged to be married to Joseph, but before they came together, she was found to be pregnant through the Holy Spirit" (Matt. 1:18 NIV).

Popular Dynamic Equivalence Versions: New International Version (NIV), New Living Translation (NLT), New Revised Standard Version (NRSV), and New English Translation (NET).

Optimal Equivalence Method: Balance of Word and Thought

Translator's Goal: Find the optimal balance between the formal and dynamic methods. When the word-for-word translation clearly states the author's original meaning, translators default to this method. When, however, they feel the word-for-word translation causes modern readers to misunderstand the author's true meaning, they defer to the thought-for-thought method.

Reader Benefits: The optimal equivalence method tends to produce a faithful translation of the original inspired text while also being easier for modern readers and those new to the Bible to understand.

Reader Challenges: At times, translators must interpret the passage, which opens the door to possible misinterpretations.

Matthew 1:18 Optimal Equivalence Example: "The birth of Jesus Christ came about this way: After his mother Mary had been engaged to Joseph, it was discovered before they came together that she was pregnant from the Holy Spirit" (Matt. 1:18 CSB).

Popular Optimal Equivalence Versions: Christian Standard Bible (CSB) and Holman Christian Standard Bible (HCSB).

Free-Thought Method: Paraphrase

Translator's Goal: Use modern lingo to express the meaning of the biblical text.

Reader Benefits: Paraphrases tend to produce a text that is the easiest to read. They can be helpful if the reader approaches them as an overview, commentary, or modern retelling of a Bible story.

Reader Challenges: Paraphrases are often more of a modern interpretation than a faithful translation. This method results in Bible versions that range from minimal interpretation of the original meaning to full freedom of expression that veers far from the inspired text and muddies its true meaning.

Compare an optimal equivalence translation of Matthew 5:14 with a paraphrase:

> "You are the light of the world.
> A city situated on a hill cannot
> be hidden." (Matt. 5:14 CSB)

> "You're here to be light, bringing out the
> God-colors in the world." (Matt. 5:14 MSG)

The Message text sounds lyrical, but what are "God-colors"? This translation muddies the original message. The

CSB sticks close to the original text and keeps the verse's meaning clear.

Matthew 1:18 Paraphrase Example: "The birth of Jesus took place like this. His mother, Mary, was engaged to be married to Joseph. Before they enjoyed their wedding night, Joseph discovered she was pregnant. (It was by the Holy Spirit, but he didn't know that)" (Matt. 1:18 MSG).

Some Popular Paraphrase Versions: Good News Translation (GNT), Contemporary English Version (CEV), The Living Bible (TLB), and The Message (MSG).

Buyer Beware: A version of the Bible with the word "Translation" in its title does not automatically make it a Bible or a true translation. It may instead be one person's thoughts on what the Bible says. When choosing a Bible, consider versions translated and edited by a team rather than an individual.

Bible Translations versus Bible Versions

The terms *translation* and *version* are often used synonymously, but they're not the same.

Translations are the original Scriptures translated into another language. A Bible's translation is typically indicated by the initials on the spine, cover, or title page, such as CSB (Christian Standard Bible), NASB (New American Standard Bible), ESV (English Standard Version), and NKJV (New King James Version).

Versions are a Bible with accessories such as study notes, articles, journaling spaces, and devotional thoughts to help us apply the truths. They can also be versions of the Bible ordered in unique ways such as chronological Bibles or one-year Bibles.

When we buy a version of the Bible, we choose the available translation we want.

By the way, a storybook Bible is not a Bible. It's a collection of specifically selected stories from the Bible for children—usually written in a paraphrase to retell the biblical account in age-appropriate ways. Storybook Bibles can be a great way to introduce young people to God's Word.

Which Bible Is Best for Me?

As someone who owns a growing collection of Bibles, I'm tempted to change the question to: "Which Bibles—plural—are best for me?" My answer is: the Bible you'll faithfully read that's faithful to God's original inspired text. It's not either/or. It's both. I also use online Bibles and Bible apps almost daily to look up and study verses and listen to the text read out loud.

Any time we spend lingering in God's Word and working to study and understand it will reap us blessings today and eternal rewards in heaven. When we commit to reading the Bible widely (cover to cover) and studying it deeply (verse by verse), our understanding of our triune God will grow and strengthen our faith.

Before you purchase your next Bible, consider what you'll use it for.

- **Studying the Bible?** Consider a study Bible in a word-for-word or optimal equivalence translation.
- **Daily Bible reading?** Consider a thought-for-thought or optimal equivalence translation of a Bible.
- **Teaching a Bible study?** You might like a word-for-word or optimal equivalence translation with wide margins for your teaching notes.
- **Teaching children?** Carefully study the passage in a word-for-word or optimal equivalence translation. Then, if needed, consult a free-thought version to help present the story in language children will understand.
- **Heading to church?** Consider a thin-line Bible of the translation your pastor uses. (Don't forget to pack your favorite method for taking notes.)

Whichever Bible we choose, our most important choice is to read it, believe it, and respond to it with obedience.

"Sanctify them by the truth; your word is truth." (John 17:17)

CHAPTER 11

AN EASY AND EFFECTIVE WAY TO STUDY THE BIBLE

GOD'S WORD NEVER CHANGES, never fails, and never becomes irrelevant because it's eternal truth. Contrary to popular opinion, we don't each have our own truths. We have beliefs we think are true, but our beliefs are only true if they agree with the Truth—with the Word of God. Truth never changes because Truth is a person—our unchangeable (immutable) Lord, Jesus Christ.

> "I am the way, and the truth,
> and the life." (John 14:6)

The Transformational Bible Study Method is an easy and effective way to study the Bible because it leads us to correctly understand the truth and rightly respond to it using three simple questions.

1. **Intent:** *What was the author's intent to his original audience?*

2. **Truth:** *What truths does God's Word reveal about the character, nature, and ways of God, and that of anyone or anything other than God?*

3. **Transformation:** *If I truly believe what God has revealed in this passage, how will the motivations and attitudes of my heart transform and my actions be different tomorrow?*

1. Intent

What was the author's intent to his original audience?

No prophecy ever came by the will
of man; instead, men spoke from
God as they were carried along by
the Holy Spirit. (2 Pet. 1:21)

The Bible's authors wrote *for* us, not *to* us. We're not their original audience. Each wrote under the leading of the Holy Spirit to a specific audience who lived in an ancient time and culture—a time and culture very different from ours.

The intent question places us into the ancient audience's sandals and leads us to read the Bible in its proper context. It guards us from inadvertently imposing our modern mindset onto the passage and thereby making Scripture mean something God never intended. Knowing a passage's context helps us better understand what we're reading because we notice details and truths we might otherwise have missed. Context matters.

Cultural Context

Culture drives much of our behavior. I live in a city with a small flower garden and a cat. The earliest Israelites were shepherds and farmers. For forty years in the wilderness, they were wandering nomads. I miss nuances in the Bible's references to their culture that the ancient audience naturally grasped. We'd likely all miss important truths if we didn't remind ourselves as we study that our world differs vastly from theirs.

Our culture would likely confuse and shock the Bible's authors. It confuses and shocks most of us. Likewise, much of their world shocks us—like picking up stones to kill someone. Even in their day, Israel's culture differed greatly from the rest of the world's. God commanded His people to worship one God (Him) and to live in holiness before Him and each other. Their neighbors worshipped many gods (all false) and embraced the sins God hated, like sacrificing their children to appease their lifeless and powerless gods.

Different times. Different cultures. Different practices. If we assume the ancients thought and acted like we do, we're going to misinterpret what we're reading. We need to consider cultural context questions like these:

- What common cultural practices of the original audience do we see in the passage?

- How did their practices influence how
  they received the author's message?
- What was the family structure like?
  Their community life?
- How did the surrounding nations' cul-
  ture influence God's people?
- What was acceptable to them but unac-
  ceptable to other cultures?
- How did God address cultural issues?

Historical Context

Israel has a storied history. Their past influenced the culture which influenced their behavior which drove how and what God inspired the authors to write.

When King David ruled Israel, the people worshipped the Lord, and God blessed them. After David died, few of Israel's kings followed his example.

Under David and his son Solomon's rule, Israel was the envy of the world. The Queen of Sheba traveled a great distance to see if the extravagant rumors were true. (They were.) Later, Israel was a laughingstock. An embarrassment. A nation dragged off like fish in a net to Babylon. In their rebellion and sin, they'd forfeited God's blessings and reaped curses—but first God sent them prophets to warn them.

Before the cross, Israel had to come to God for forgive-ness of their sins with the proper sacrifice—the one that pointed to Christ. Without the shedding of blood there was no forgiveness of sin (Heb. 9:22). On the cross, Christ ended the sacrificial system. He was the perfect and final sacrifice for all sin. Forgiveness comes through faith in Christ alone.

Historical context questions like the following help us better interpret what we're reading:

- What was happening in history at the time this book was written?
- What historical framework did Israel have for their understanding of God and His commands?
- What laws, promises, and warnings of God did the people have to live by at the time the author wrote?
- What were the audience's leaders like? Godly? Evil?
- What were the surrounding nations like?
- Did the audience live before or after the flood? Before or after God's people went into captivity? Before or after Jesus died on the cross?

Grammatical Context

The Bible's authors wrote in Greek, Hebrew, and Aramaic. Their ancient sentence structures, idioms, and lingo can be hard for us to decipher—even after they're translated into our language.

For instance, consider Jesus's words to the Jewish leaders in John 8:58: "Truly I tell you, before Abraham was, I am." His words may seem odd to us but not inflammatory. Confusing, but not offensive. Jesus's listeners took great offense. They picked up stones to kill Him. They understood Jesus's use of the phrase "I am" was a clear and obvious claim to be God.

As we read, we want to ask ourselves what the literal context is—what the clear and obvious meaning of each verse was to the author's audience. To help us determine the usual and customary sense of the text in the author's day, we need to consider aspects of the grammatical context such as verb conjugation, sentence structure, and genre.

Each genre of literature follows their own rules for interpretation. Verb tenses can change the meaning of a verse. Whether a word is singular or plural can also change the meaning. Grammatical context matters. But fear not! Wiser scholars than us can help us understand these through dictionaries, concordances, and commentaries as we consider questions like these:

- What genre did the author use in this passage? Did he write narrative (story), law, poetry, wisdom literature, epistles (letters), or prophecy?
- Are there ancient idioms, lingo, and writing styles in the passage we need to consider?
- Is the word singular or plural?
- Is the verb past, present, or future tense? Or continuous tense?
- What's the full range of meaning that this original Hebrew or Greek word carries, and when considering it in a

particular passage, which of those meanings makes the most sense taken in
context?

• How does the passage fit into the surrounding verses and chapter? The whole
book? The overarching story of the Bible?

If these many intent questions overwhelm you, don't
panic. As we ease into studying the Bible, our first step is
to simply recognize and remember that we're modern people
reading an ancient text. Context matters. Understanding the
various contexts and background information in each book
will come in time.

2. Truth

**What truths does God's Word reveal about
the character, nature, and ways of God,
and that of anyone or anything other than God?**

May grace and peace be multiplied to
you through the knowledge of God
and of Jesus our Lord. (2 Pet. 1:2)

I said before that the Bible was written *for* us, not *to* us.
It's also true that while the Bible is *for* us, it's not *about* us.
God gave us the Bible so we can know and glorify Him, not
ourselves. No other truths transform us more than knowing
God and knowing the character, nature, and ways of the
Father, Son, and Holy Spirit.

Each page of the Bible opens a window into the radiant glory of God, showing us His character, nature, and ways. The Holy Spirit works through the truths in God's Word to grow us spiritually and make our reflection resemble Christ's more and more.

> "Sanctify them by the truth; your
> word is truth." (John 17:17)

We ask fewer questions in this step, but the few we ask are life-changing.

- What does our triune God reveal about Himself in the passage?
- How do we see the presence or work of the Father, Son, or the Holy Spirit?
- What does God reveal about the world, sin, Satan, or anyone or anything else in the passage?
- What promises, truths, or commands of God is the author communicating?

3. Transformation

If I truly believe what God has revealed in this passage, how will the motivations and attitudes of my heart transform and my actions be different tomorrow?

> For the word of God is living and
> effective and sharper than any double-
> edged sword, penetrating as far as the

> separation of soul and spirit, joints and
> marrow. It is able to judge the thoughts
> and intentions of the heart. (Heb. 4:12)

God gave us the Bible for *transformation*, not simply *information*. God's Word works more like a surgeon's scalpel than a library of knowledge. Scripture performs open-heart surgery on our attitudes and motivations and exposes what we truly know and believe. When we believe the truth we learn in God's Word, the truth replaces the lies and transforms our hearts and minds—and moves us to action.

Answering the transformation question helps us identify the many ways a heart changed by God naturally responds to truth. If our belief doesn't move our hands and feet to respond, it's not true belief. It's simply knowledge. True belief responds with action. "Faith without works is dead" (James 2:26).

Our answers to the transformation question help us recognize the weaknesses in our faith so we can confess them and fix our hearts and minds on knowing and believing the Truth. Then, and only then, will our faith be transformed and Spirit-led actions flow out to God's glory.

Can versus Will

An important aspect of the transformation step is understanding the subtle but powerful difference between *can* and *will* and between *doing* and *responding*.

Let me explain.

For many years, I misapplied the popular Bible study question, "How does this verse apply to my life?" I inadvertently turned the application step of Bible study into a self-improvement exercise. I made it about my *doing* rather than my *responding*. About what I *can* do versus what I *will* do if I truly believe God's Word.

Doing focuses on ourselves and our ability to obey God—to apply His Word to our lives. We hear a truth, and we make a conscious effort to do it. We acknowledge we *can* obey Him. This is good and true. However, considering how true faith responds is even better.

Responding keeps the focus on God and His power at work in us. We hear the transformational truth of God's Word and respond to it out of a changed heart (Phil. 2:13). We *will* obey.

I'm not saying we don't have to choose to obey God's Word. We're called to obey whether we believe God's commands or not. I'm saying that if we truly believe, it's not just that we *can* choose to obey God, we *will* choose to obey Him.

When we don't obey, or we struggle to obey, the struggle reveals a weakness in our faith. After all, if we truly believed everything the Bible reveals about who God is, we'd respond in holy obedience every time—like Jesus did.

The more we believe the truth, the more we'll naturally love what God loves and hate what He hates. Our hearts will more naturally overflow with a desire for His will, rather than our own.

When we answer the transformation question, we help ourselves understand what it looks like to truly believe God's Word. As we study the Bible, we want to determine not what we *can* do if we truly believe God's Word, but what we *will* do.

We can then use this description of a Christlike response to the truths we read and compare it to how we're currently responding—or reacting.

Are we living like we say we believe?

Do our actions and thoughts match the description of Christlike transformation we noted?

If not, why?

Faith Alert Notifications

Whenever our gut reactions to the transformation question don't match our answers, we're alerted to an area where we need God to grow our faith. We need to ask God to reveal the truth of why our actions and thoughts don't match our description of Christlike transformation.

If we say we believe God is sovereign and controls all things, yet we still worry all the time, we need to ask God why. Do we truly believe He's sovereign? Or do we not yet fully trust God *in* His sovereignty. Perhaps we're not convinced He's always good—at least always good to us. We can surprise ourselves at how many truths about God we think we believe only to discover we actually struggle to believe them. Or we don't yet fully understand them.

Our struggle may also be our pride. Like Adam and Eve in the garden, we want to be the one in control. We want God to submit to us on at least a few matters—like our hopes, dreams, and closest relationships.

This common struggle with pride leads us back to unbelief. Like Adam and Eve when they doubted God, somewhere a seed of doubt sprouted. We need the truth to expose and root out the doubt. Lingering over the transformation question helps.

God's Spirit will move our hearts toward true change as we ask searching questions like these:

- If I truly believe God's Word in this passage, what will this look like in my life?
- Is there something I don't yet know about God that I need to know?
- Is there unbelief I need to confess? A sin I've refused to forsake? An unbiblical thought I've let nest in my mind?
- Is my pride refusing to humble itself in obedience to God's authority over my life?
- What does it look like for me to worship God in light of the truths in this passage?

Do not be conformed to this age, but
be transformed by the renewing of
your mind, so that you may discern
what is the good, pleasing, and
perfect will of God. (Rom. 12:2)

Transformational Bible Study Method Example

As an example of how this method works, let's consider the first half of Habakkuk 1:12:

Are you not from everlasting,
O LORD my God, my Holy One?
We shall not die. (ESV)

Intent

A brief reading of an introduction to Habakkuk gives us important background information. We learn that Habakkuk was a prophet who ministered to the southern kingdom of Judah during one of Israel's most perilous times in history.

Judah had long since stopped following the Lord and had been abusing their own people with violence. Habakkuk begged God to stop them as He had done in the past. God responded with news that made Habakkuk's knees wobble. God announced He was raising up the terrifying nation of Babylon to judge Judah. Verse 12 is Habakkuk's gut reaction to God's news.

Truth

Habakkuk's knee-jerk reaction to God's terrifying news was to center himself on at least four unshakable truths he knew about God:

1. **God is everlasting.** He never changes. From eternity to eternity, He is forever the same.
2. **God is the Lord—He's *Yahweh*.** Yahweh is the Hebrew name God used for Himself to proclaim His desire to be in a relationship with us. It's His covenant-keeping name. Regardless of the unfaithfulness of

God's people, He's forever faithful to us
and His promises.

3. **Our Lord is God—*Elohim*.** God called
Himself *Elohim* when He created the
world (Gen. 1:1). This name proclaims
God is the supreme and sovereign God—
the all-sufficient and un-created Creator.

4. **God is the Holy One.** He's set apart,
completely different from all else. Every
attribute of His is holy and free of even
the possibility of evil.

These four truths filled Habakkuk with confidence
that even though Babylon was coming to destroy their city
and drag them into captivity, the kingdom of Judah would
not die. The people of God would not cease to exist. They
couldn't because God had promised to send a Savior—the
Messiah—through Judah. He doesn't break His promises.
Not one word of His fails. Eventually, the Messiah would
come through Judah because their everlasting and holy God
keeps His covenants. Even in His judgment, God sustains
His people.

Transformation

If we truly believe these four truths Habakkuk declared,
our confidence in the Lord will be strengthened even in the
face of terrifying news, particularly because, compared to
Habbakuk's place in history, we stand on the other side of
the cross. He had God's promise that a Savior would come.
We have the fulfillment. Christ has come, and He gives

Christians eternal life and His indwelling Spirit to empower us to stand strong. Just like Judah, we will not die—because we have been granted not just staying power through trials, but resurrection life on the other side of this world's story. Our knees may wobble when calamity comes, but we will not despair. We'll walk in the strength of the Lord—if we truly believe in God's Word through Habakkuk.

If we truly believe these truths, we'll submit every fear to the truth we know, confident that neither God nor truth change. We'll rest in God's unbreakable and holy promises and ways—even when we don't understand them. We'll stand firm, confident that God will either sustain us in or lead us out of our trials. Or He'll bring us into His eternal presence with great joy. We will know that we will not die—at least not eternally.

Four Extra Bible Study Tips

Tip #1: Pay attention to the little guys— conjunctions and prepositions.

Conjunctions and prepositions may seem insignificant, but they play an important role in Bible study. These connecting and linking words direct and clarify the important message that follows them. These little words reveal vital aspects of God's message that we might miss.

- **Conjunctions** connect words, phrases, and ideas together with linking words like *therefore, as, but, because, even though,* *nevertheless, and, as, but, now, so, that, when*, and *while*.

— Whenever we read the word *therefore*, ask what the *therefore* is there for.

~ Whatever comes before the word *therefore* is the key to understanding the message after it.

~ The key to understanding the message that comes after the word *therefore* is found in whatever came before it.

~ When the word *therefore* comes at the beginning of a chapter, we must back up and read the passages in the chapter before it.

— The conjunction *but* can change everything. Whenever we come across this word, pause and consider how the author is moving our thinking into a new direction.

• **Prepositions** introduce phrases that draw the reader's attention to important details like direction, time, location, or purpose. Prepositions are words like *under, because of, that, with, in, by, at, to, on, in, since, for, about, during, until*, and *after*.

— Make a habit of slowing down when you see a preposition and considering what important detail the author is highlighting. This information may seem trivial or even boring—until we pay attention to them. Then we realize their importance.

Tip #2: Watch for repeats.

Every word in the Bible was carefully chosen. No word is random or insignificant. When the author used repeated words, phrases, ideas, and themes, he wasn't being lazy or redundant. He repeated to grab his audience's attention. He echoed his messages for emphasis. As you read the Bible, pay attention for repeats. Watch for the author's repetitions. They matter. (Did you see what I did there?)

Tip #3: Notice chapter and verse breaks.

Most of the Bible's authors intended for us to read their books (or letters) as one continuous text. They didn't insert chapter or verse breaks. Fortunately for us, wise men inserted them centuries later so we can quickly and easily find a specific passage or verse. As great as this convenience is, it also creates some challenges.

Chapter and verse breaks inadvertently interrupt the text's flow and distance it from its full context. This distance can lead us to wrongly assume the breaks indicate a change in thought, time, or events and cause us to misinterpret God's intended message. We might think the prior and/or following text are unrelated to each other. Let's enjoy the verse and chapter breaks but beware of their pitfalls.

Tip #4: Doubt yourself, not God or His Word.

If you read anything in a faithful translation of the Bible that seems to contradict something else in the Bible or makes God look bad, stop and remind yourself of the truth.[1] God is perfect. He's never the author of evil. He cannot lie or contradict Himself. Likewise, God's Word is perfect. It's trustworthy and true.

If we don't like something God has said or done in His Word or we read an apparent contradiction, the problem isn't with God or the Bible. It's with us.

We may need to learn something we don't understand about God or about the situation in the text. As we learn more about the Bible and how to properly study and interpret it, the more our understanding rises and "contradictions" fall away.

It may also be that our pride is tempting us to doubt God and/or reject the truth we know—like pride did to Adam and Eve, Israel, the disciples, and every other human on earth.

We have innumerable reasons to doubt our doubts (such as our limited knowledge and wisdom), but we have no reasons to doubt our infinite and wise God or His faithful Word.

> Trust in the LORD with all your heart,
> and do not rely on your own understanding;
> in all your ways know him, and he will
> make your paths straight. (Prov. 3:5–6)

Bible Study Is a Life-Changing Adventure

Bible study that leads to transformation is one of life's greatest adventures. The joy of discovering and being transformed (sanctified) by the treasures and promises of God's Word far surpasses any other discovery. As we come to know God more, the riches of His grace and peace will multiply in our hearts beyond all measure.

I rejoice over your promise
like one who finds vast
treasure. (Ps. 119:162)

CHAPTER 12

DOCTRINE: STRAITJACKET OR LIFE VEST?

THE FIRST TIME I met with my mentor, Grace, she said, "Sit down, Jean. We're going to study doctrine."

Images flashed through my mind of dusty old books filled with words like *propitiation* and *imputation*. I groaned—inwardly, of course. I didn't want her to know I was already bored.

The word *doctrine* sounded like a straitjacket, designed to hold me in bondage to outdated beliefs no longer relevant in "today's Christianity." I'd asked Grace to meet with me because I wanted to love God and His Word more, not study doctrine or other stifling religious trappings.

Then I learned the truth: Doctrine is desirable and inescapable for Christians.

Doctrine is desirable because it encapsulates the teachings and principles of the Bible that direct our lives and mature us (Eph. 4:14–16).[1]

Doctrine is inescapable because anyone who knows about the Bible holds beliefs about what it teaches—about its doctrines—even if they can't put a name to them (like *regeneration* and *justification*).

As Christians, our concern is to know whether the doctrines we already believe (knowingly or unknowingly) are true or false.

Scripture Determines Doctrine

Doctrine is "a body of beliefs about God, humankind, Christ, the church, and other related concepts considered authoritative and thus worthy of acceptance by all members of the community of faith."[2]

In short, doctrine pulls the threaded truths from every corner of the Bible and ties them together into words, phrases, and categories like *atonement* or the *deity of Christ*.

Sadly, many churches today are like the Pharisees of Jesus's day. He criticized them for teaching as doctrine what Scripture does not teach (Mark 7:1–8).

People don't determine biblical doctrine. God does through His Word.

As we study the Bible, we learn the doctrines God established. His teachings shape our beliefs, rather than our molding His teachings to shape what we want to believe—or what our culture tells us to believe.

Faithful Bible study leads to sound doctrine. The original Greek word for "sound" is *hygiainousēs*, which is where we get our English word for *hygiene*. We want our doctrine to be so sound it's clean of all impurities of false teaching.

Sound doctrine rises out of good *theology*—the study of God's character, nature, and ways. Like doctrine, theology is inescapable. As Dr. R. C. Sproul said, "Every Christian is a theologian. Perhaps not a theologian in the technical or professional sense, but a theologian, nevertheless. The issue for Christians is not whether we are going to be theologians but whether we are going to be good theologians or bad ones."[3]

Sadly, some of the biggest churches in the world boldly teach false doctrines based on theology they developed from their culture. Many churches have changed their beliefs on marriage, sexuality, the Bible's inerrancy, and many other truths. They've caved to the world's beliefs stating as one pastor said, "As culture changes, we must change with it."

Too many churches twist and redefine Scripture to make it more palatable (and *sellable*) to the world—and to themselves. Just as Paul warned, "For the time will come when people will not tolerate sound doctrine, but according to their own desires, will multiply teachers for themselves because they have an itch to hear what they want to hear. They will turn away from hearing the truth and will turn aside to myths" (2 Tim. 4:3–4).

Knowing Sound Doctrine Isn't Automatic

For several years, Lifeway Research has conducted a "State of Theology" study, examining what people believe about several biblical doctrines.[4] In each survey, the results revealed a widespread and shocking lack of understanding of what the Bible truly teaches, even among those who attend church regularly.

This study reinforces the fact that while we all hold beliefs about the Bible, knowing and believing sound doctrine isn't automatic. We need to do the work and study the Bible to learn its teachings ourselves.

If we don't know what the Bible truly teaches, we can unknowingly mix the world's beliefs in with the Bible's true teachings. Well-meaning Christians can get caught up in the riptide of emotions as they react to culture's cries and swept into every kind of wrong belief. Well-packaged lies can feel truer than the Truth.

The risks of ignoring doctrine are too great. Our salvation might even be at stake because if the gospel we believed isn't the true gospel, our belief, no matter how sincere, won't save us. There's only one true gospel (1 Cor. 15:1–10; Gal. 1:6–12).

With all this danger lurking, is it time to panic?

Fortunately, no. God has given us His Word. The Bible is our strong and unfailing life vest, not a straitjacket. Knowing doctrine keeps us from sinking into confusion and erroneous teaching. Knowing doctrine keeps us buoyed in the truth.

Doctrinal Terms Make Life Easier

You may be wondering if we can leave the tongue-twisting doctrinal terms such as *eschatology* or *ecclesiology* to seminary students? We could, but putting a name to a face (or a term to a doctrine) makes life easier.

For instance, when Grace noticed my tendency toward worry, she said, "Jean, do you know why you worry so much?"

"Because life is scary?"

"No," she said. "Because you don't trust God's sovereignty."

"His what?"

Grace sat me beside her, opened her Bible, and flipped through the Scriptures. She showed me multiple passages that teach this vital peace-giving doctrine. In that hour and many more afterward, Grace taught me how trusting in the sovereignty of the Lord destroys fear, worry, anxiety, and all their fretting cousins.

I can encapsulate what Grace taught me from Scripture in seventy-eight words:

> God's sovereignty means that He is in control of everything and has been since eternity. He orchestrates all things by His holy power and wisdom.
>
> Nothing can touch our lives without His express permission. He never commits evil nor entices anyone to do evil, but even Satan and the worst scourges of humanity can't move an inch without God allowing them.
>
> God does whatever He wants with whoever He wants whenever He wants for whatever purpose He wants.

I used seventy-eight words to summarize what two words (and one doctrine) teach: *God's sovereignty.*

Grace's definition made me shudder at first. Her statement, "God does whatever He wants with whoever He wants whenever He wants for whatever purpose He wants," sounds like the perfect mantra for a bully. But then I remembered what Grace taught me through the Bible about God's holiness, goodness, love, and wisdom.

God's *holiness* assures us that His desire is always good and free of even the hint of evil. His *goodness* assures us that everything He does is always pure and right. When we cap these off with the doctrines of God's *love, wisdom, omniscience* (that He's all-knowing), and *immutability* (that He can never change), we're resting well tonight.

It would take me a full chapter to describe the beauty of these attributes and doctrines of God. I'm glad we can sum each up in only a word or two. I'm even more grateful that my mentor taught me the importance of knowing the doctrines of the Bible.

Don't Get Overwhelmed—Get Started

There's an endless list of concerns that could rob us of sleep for the rest of our lives and leave us treading in turbulent waters to the end of our days. Or we can hold fast to the life vest of true biblical doctrine and enjoy peace.

The goal of doctrine isn't to provide Christians with an impressive new vocabulary. It's to transform our hearts, renew our minds, and spill out into our hands and feet through Christ-like service.

So how many doctrines do we need to learn?

All of them. Over time.

Don't get overwhelmed. Get started.

May I suggest diving into the first doctrine Grace taught me—the doctrine of God. Study who He is and what He does through the Scriptures. Study the Father, Son, and Holy Spirit and their attributes, nature, and ways.

Then maybe study the doctrine of God's Revelation, which is His Word. (I'm not referring to the last book of the Bible, although the book of Revelation is also important to study.) Study the Bible's inspiration, inerrancy, authority, and clarity. These truths infuse us with confidence that we can understand the Bible, believe it, and live by it with enduring joy and peace.

Each week I returned to Grace's house for more doctrinal training, and I was never bored. Instead, each week I fell more in love with God and His Word.

Imagine that.

CHAPTER 13

WHY CHURCH MATTERS

IF I HAVE A Bible, do I need the church?

Yes.

How's that for a simple answer?

Our next question requires a fuller answer.

Why do we need the church?

Before we talk about why we need the church, let's first define what we mean by "the church."

What Is the Church?

Before Christ went to the cross, He promised His disciples He wouldn't leave them alone. He said the Father would send the Holy Spirit, and He'd build His church—*the* church.[1] After Christ returned to heaven, the Holy Spirit came to the believers gathered in Jerusalem on the Jewish festival of Pentecost, and the church took form.[2] Now, no matter where you travel in the world, when you meet another Christian, you're meeting a member of your family. Another member of the church Christ died to save.

But what is the church?

The church is the body of believers and the family of God. Christ calls her His bride.[3] The church is every soul who's trusted in Jesus since the garden of Eden. The English word *church* originated from the Greek word *ekklesia*, which means "gathering" or "assembly." This word gives us a vital component of every church—the gathering together of Christ's family to worship the Lord and be equipped for service.

Pastor Bernard Howard explains: "In every New Testament usage, while *ekklesia* can mean *more* than a gathering, it never means something *unrelated to* a gathering. The most important gathering in the New Testament is the gathering of all Christians around Jesus in heaven—an assembly that's already in place . . . Think of those TV shows where a character turns to the camera to speak directly to the audience. It's as if the character is simultaneously in two worlds: the world of the show and the world of the audience. Christians similarly 'turn to the camera' whenever we remind ourselves that we belong to Jesus's heavenly assembly and are here on earth as its ambassadors."[4]

Christ loves the church, but she's not perfect since she's made of imperfect people. Like the institution of marriage, though, the church is God's perfect design for His people.[5] As a bride longs to be with her husband, we, the church, long to be with Christ. Until we can be with Him face-to-face in heaven, we're with Him through His indwelling Holy Spirit, His Word, prayer, and His people—the church. The *visible* and the *invisible* church.

The Visible and Invisible Church

When people ask, "What church do you belong to?" they're not talking about the worldwide body of believers. They're asking which local congregation of believers you joined—or attend.

When they ask, "Where is your church?" they mean, "Where is your church's building?"

In other words, they're asking about the *visible* church.

The *visible* church is the building along with both the Christians and non-Christians who attend weekly services and events.

The *invisible* church is the true church—all who belong to Christ by faith. Christians.[6]

Not every person who attends church is a Christian. They may be sitting in a church service, but not a member of the invisible church. The Holy Spirit may have drawn them to the service. Or perhaps a family member, friend, or the desire to appear spiritual dragged them to church.

Some people know they're not a Christian. Tragically, some think they are, but they've never actually believed the gospel. Either way, they're in the best place if they're in a faithful church because they'll hear the good news of Jesus Christ that's able to save their souls and adopt them into the family of God, the invisible church.[7]

As you search for a church, look for one with the characteristics of a faithful church.

Characteristics of a Faithful Church

The size of a church doesn't necessarily indicate that it's faithful to the Bible. It may only indicate the church's ability to draw a crowd. As you visit churches, don't let the size of the congregation influence you. Faithful and unfaithful churches come in all sizes. Instead, look for a church that worships the Lord by holding firmly to God's design for His church set out in the New Testament, starting with Matthew 28:19–20, Ephesians 4, 1 and 2 Timothy, and Titus.

A faithful church equips the saints for how to live in this world as Christians who exalt and honor Christ in all they do. The gospel permeates their services and activities.

The leaders disciple their members to follow Christ, teaching them the Bible so they can know Christ better and obey His Word. They celebrate the Lord's Supper as a body and baptize believers as a public confession of their faith in Christ.

The members pray for each other, serve each other, and in humility and love, hold each other accountable to grow in spiritual maturity. They remember the poor among them and love and forgive as Christ has loved and forgiven them.

And they hold a high view of God and His Word, starting with the leadership. As the leadership goes, so go the members. Our leaders should strive to be like Christ, but they're not going to be perfect in this world. They can, however—and must—hold a high view of God and His Word. This cannot be overstated. But what does this look like?

Leaders with a high view of God and His Word . . .

- Submit themselves to the authority of God's Word, trusting that God faithfully communicated His Word through divine inspiration and has preserved it throughout the ages.
- Affirm and hold to Scripture as the infallible and inerrant source of all truth, able to meet every spiritual and emotional need.
- Follow God's command in 1 Timothy 3:4–5 by taking care of their own families with gentleness and intentional presence.
- Focus their sermons and worship music on the character of God, the exaltation of Christ and His gospel (rather than exalting man), and the truths found in Scripture.
- Commit to preaching God's Word, rather than unbiblical cultural norms, even at the risk of offending unbelievers and popular leaders.
- Trust the Holy Spirit and the preaching of God's Word to draw hearers to confess and turn from sin and surrender to Christ rather than rely on special effects, dramatic music, or cleverly worded messages to play on the listeners' emotions.

- Trust God to meet all their needs in His timing and ways rather than manipulate others to get what they want.
- Don't exalt the pastor or foster a "rock star" mentality around leadership in the church, whether that be preaching leaders or worship leaders.
- Lead the church and hold each other accountable by a plurality of leadership—elders, shepherds, pastors, and deacons. (Different churches use different names for these roles.) This allows for checks and balances in the church's leadership structure instead of all decisions and power remaining in the jurisdiction of one person.
- Maintain a culture of grace, openness, and submission to God's will and authority rather than a permissive or defensive posture, especially when questioned or criticized.
- Commit to practicing corporate and personal holiness, and when necessary, church discipline to restore an unrepentant member into fellowship.
- Willing to endure criticism and persecution to honor God, obey His Word, and care for Christ's bride, the church.

How to Find a Faithful Local Church

As you begin your search, the following church locators and internet search suggestion may help you find a faithful church in your area. Not every great church will necessarily appear on one of these lists. Talk with everyone you meet. Ask where they go to church and why. Their responses may reveal that their church holds a high view of God—or that it doesn't.

- **9Marks Church Locator:** 9marks.org/church-search
- **G3 Ministry Find a Church:** g3min.org/g3-church-network/map
- **The Gospel Coalition Church Directory:** thegospelcoalition.org/churches
- **The Master's Seminary Find a Church Locator:** tms.edu/find-a-church
- **Type in your internet search bar:** "Churches in my area that teach the Bible verse-by-verse" aka "practice expository preaching." (Churches that preach verse-by-verse tend to have a high view of God. I explain this type of preaching below.)

As you create a list of potential churches, visit their worship service and notice how they treat the Bible. Since God's Word has the final say on what we're to believe and how we're to live, we need to know what the Bible teaches. Does the Bible take center stage in their service? Is the worship music focused on expressing scriptural truth? Does the sermon teach the Bible in such a way that you clearly understand the passage and know how to respond to it in worship? Do you leave the service knowing how to live out the truths you've learned or only with a good feeling and a funny story?

Consider the Holy Spirit's example. He never draws attention to Himself. He always points us to Christ. If a sermon focuses more on what we can get from the Lord than on who God is and what He's done, beware. Sermons should move us to worship and serve Christ and others, not exalt ourselves, or exalt a leader or ministry.

Consider looking for a church that preaches the Bible verse-by-verse—a church that practices *expository* or *expositional* preaching. These two words refer to preaching that pulls out of Scripture the message God gave His authors to communicate. This kind of preaching walks us through God's Word verse-by-verse to open the eyes of our understanding to the inspired Scriptures and its glorious truths. Properly done, it helps us translate these truths into responses that grow us into Christlike love and deeds in a world that's increasingly hostile to Christ and His church.

Expository preaching used to be the norm, but it's becoming harder to find. The more our culture demands to be entertained, the more the modern churches' leaders have obliged. The job of the pastor isn't to entertain the masses, but to equip its members. The equipping we need most is a faithful understanding of the Bible. It alone holds the words of life and how to live in this world.

When you find a faithful local church, join it.

Note, I didn't say a *perfect* church. Perfect churches don't exist because people are imperfect, and people make up the church.

What If You Can't Find a Faithful Church?

Depending on where you live, you may have a hundred local churches to choose between or none. What do you do if you can't find a faithful church near you?

First, pray and trust Christ. He's the head of the church. Trust Him to guide you. Trust Him throughout your entire church journey. People fail. He never does.

If your community is small and has few options, you're most likely not the only person looking for a church with a high view of God. Attend Sunday school classes or Small Groups (sometimes called Home Groups, Life Groups, Community Groups, etc.). Talk with their members. You may find a group of Christians within a church who are truly devoted to teaching and living out God's Word.

Visit several times before you make a decision—unless the church clearly teaches lies or glorifies their pastor or money. Then move on. Quickly.

God will provide, but it may take time. And you might have to drive. Our church has members who drive an hour. The church is our spiritual family. Finding one devoted to sound biblical teaching and each other is worth the search and the drive.

Whatever you do, don't stay home as some were in the habit of doing in the early days of the church and is common still today.[8]

We Desperately Need the Church

We can always find excuses to walk away from the church, starting with the many flawed people who attend it, like me. But how can we when God has commanded us not to give up meeting together with the local body of believers? We need the church. We desperately need her. Pastor C. H. Spurgeon shared some profound reasons why:

> Now I know there are some who say, "Well, I hope I have given myself to the Lord, but I do not intend to give myself to any church, because____." Now why not? "Because I can be a Christian without it." Now are you quite clear about that? You can be as good a Christian by disobedience to your Lord's commands as by being obedient? . . .
>
> There is a brick—a very good one. What is the brick made for? To help to build a house with. It is of no use for that brick to tell you that it is just as good a brick while it is kicking about on the ground as it would be in the house. It is a good-for-nothing brick! Until it is built into the wall, it is no good! So you rolling-stone Christians, I do not believe that you are answering your purpose—you

are living contrary to the life which Christ would have you live—and you are much to blame for the injury you do![9]

Did this last part of Spurgeon's quote sting a little? Remember, God didn't create us to be alone, and when Christ returned to heaven, He didn't leave us alone. He sent us His Holy Spirit to live in us, and He gave us the church. We hurt ourselves if we stay away from the church, and likewise, we injure our sisters and brothers in Christ when we stay home.

In a time when we can watch worship services online in our living room in the comfort of our pajamas, the temptation to stay home is strong. But the injury to ourselves and our Christian family is stronger.

For those with physical limitations that keep them away against their will, belonging to a local church brings our brothers and sisters to them. A faithful church takes care of its family.

Do not fall for Satan's and the world's lie. Pastor Paul David Tripp reminds us that "The enemy of our souls will do anything he can to keep us from participating fully, from hearing clearly, and from committing to God more intentionally through gathered worship."[10]

We need the church. Desperately.

When you find a faithful local church, join her and love her. Christ died for her. She's His beloved bride.

> . . . Christ loved the church and gave
> himself for her to make her holy, cleansing
> her with the washing of water by the

word. He did this to present the church
to himself in splendor, without spot
or wrinkle or anything like that, but
holy and blameless. (Eph. 5:25b–27)

CHAPTER 14

HELPFUL BIBLE STUDY TOOLS AND RESOURCES

IF YOU'RE A CHRISTIAN on a deserted island with only the text of the Bible—no cross-references, commentaries, or study notes—you have all you need to understand God's Word. The Holy Spirit doesn't need tools. He's able to teach us everything God wants us to know. But, if you're not on a deserted island, there's nothing wrong with using available tools and resources.

Before we look at the wealth of tools, let's first consider an important principle to follow when using biblical resources.

Be Bible Dependent, Not Resource Dependent

I love my collection of study Bibles, but I'm aware of how easy it is to be tempted to let them do all the work for me. Learning to study and interpret the Bible faithfully on our own is better than turning to the closest study tool the moment we stumble over a passage.

We want our tools to supplement and confirm our study, not replace it. To help us verify that our understanding of a passage is correct and not veering off into error. It's better to know how to correctly interpret Scripture ourselves rather than simply know how to read the study notes in our Bible.

Study Bibles, commentaries, and other tools are fantastic, but let's not be content with being spoon-fed the Bible's meaning forever. Besides, even the best biblical scholars aren't perfect. No pastor, teacher, or author is infallible. The number of best-selling books an author publishes is only an indication of how many people like the message, not that the message is true to the Bible. Only God's Word is perfect. The Bible remains our single best resource for learning doctrine and shaping our theology. It alone is authoritative.

Pastor and Bible teacher, Dr. Marty Minto cautions us that resource dependency leads to what he calls *second-hand theology*—theology formed from the teachings of others rather than from the Bible.[1] God wants us to develop our theology from studying the Bible, not simply from studying books about the Bible. Resources and tools bless us, but let's avoid becoming dependent on them.

Helpful Bible Study Tools and Resources

The resources below are only a small sampling of the many great tools available today. For a full list of recommended resources for each of the following tools, visit the "Ease into the Bible" resource tab on my website, JeanWilund.com.

Bibles with Study Notes (Study Bibles)

Study Bibles contain the full text of the Bible along with study notes typically at the bottom of the page commenting on many of the verses. Study Bibles often provide other great tools such as Bible book introductions, articles, cross-references, maps, and a concordance.

Study Bibles without the name of a person attached to it (such as the *CSB Study Bible*), contain notes and commentary by teams of biblical scholars.

A study Bible with the name of a person connected to it (such as the *Spurgeon Study Bible*) contains study notes and commentary gathered from the scholar's teachings.

Some study Bibles are geared by age groups and gender such as women's study Bibles, men's study Bibles, teen or student study Bibles, and so on.

Some versions focus mostly on topics or application. The notes and articles in the *Gospel Transformation Study Bible: Christ in All of Scripture, Grace for All of Life* were created by a team of theologians. The notes highlight how Christ is evident in all of Scripture and how believers today can respond to biblical truths in a transformational way.

The notes in the *Spurgeon Study Bible* by the nineteenth-century "Prince of Preachers" Charles H. Spurgeon came from his sermons. The notes focus more on how we can apply the biblical truths than on explaining the verses' meaning.

The *CSB Day-by-Day Chronological Bible* takes us through the Bible in chronological order and offers questions to ponder as we respond to God's Word.

The *Literary Study Bible* helps us understand the literary devices used in each book, while the *Cultural Study Bible* discusses each book's cultural setting. (Much of this information is also included in Bible commentaries and guides.)

The *Thompson Chain-Reference Bible* provides cross-reference verses related to eight thousand topics mentioned in the Bible.

The *Hebrew-Greek Key Word Study Bible* provides the original Hebrew or Greek of key words in the Bible and explains how they're used in the text. Knowing the original words and their full definition and use can give us better insight into the author's intended meaning.

Bible Commentaries

Bible commentaries give in-depth explanations of books of the Bible beyond what a study Bible tends to provide. Most commentaries explain every verse in a particular book(s) of the Bible.

When studying commentaries, it's important to remember—as we should with everything we read—only God's Word is inspired and infallible. When we remember this fact, we can benefit greatly from commentaries. As much as the authors strive to faithfully interpret the Bible, we can't assume their interpretation is perfect. Not even the brightest scholars all agree on the correct meaning of every verse in the Bible.

Each commentary reflects the beliefs of its author, thus, it's a good idea to read more than one when checking your own interpretation of Scripture. Fortunately, many websites and apps provide a host of great commentaries for free such as on Biblehub.com, BibleGateway.com, and BlueLetterBible.org.

Bible Dictionaries and Encyclopedias

Bible Dictionaries: Bible dictionaries, such as the *Holman Illustrated Bible Dictionary*, provide more than just the definition of words in the Bible, although this alone makes them valuable. A good one also provides information on the people, places, unfamiliar terms, cultures, and doctrines of the Bible as well as maps and photographs.

Noah Webster's 1828 English Dictionary: As we read through Scripture, we're going to stumble over English words we don't use daily, like *atonement*. Even if we can use it in a sentence, the *1828 Webster's Dictionary* helps us grasp its full meaning and reflects the Bible's definition of words. No modern English dictionary compares to the *1828 Webster's Dictionary* for studying the Bible—and it's free online at webstersdictionary1828.com. (Compare the *1828 Dictionary* entry for the word *marriage* with any modern dictionary, and you'll see what I mean.)

Bible Encyclopedias: Bible encyclopedias, such as the *Baker Encyclopedia of the Bible*, provide similar information as a dictionary but go into greater detail about every notable word, person, place, and thing in the Bible.

Bible Handbooks and Guides

Bible handbooks and guides offer a more general overview or explanation of the books of the Bible than a commentary.

Some focus on one aspect of the Bible, such as its doctrines. Others provide broader information on the Bible. *MacArthur's Quick Reference Guide to the Bible* lists a wealth of background information including the author and date it was written, the key people, words and doctrines in the book, and a quick overview. For handbooks on each of the testaments, consider *The Old Testament Handbook* or *The New Testament Handbook* (B&H Publishing Group).

Bible Reading Enhancements: Bible Studies, Devotionals, and Liturgies

Bible studies, devotionals, and liturgies aren't designed to replace our Bible reading time, but to enhance it.

Bible studies consist of prepared lessons for individuals or groups that help us grow in our understanding of the Bible and how to live it out. Some studies teach on topics while others teach a specific book (or part of a book) of the Bible. Some even teach us how to study the Bible for ourselves.

Devotionals are short messages centered around a Bible passage that focus our hearts and minds on the truth of God's Word and encourage us in our spiritual growth.

Liturgies prepare our hearts for reading the Bible. They're an outstanding addition for anyone's daily Bible reading and particularly helpful for anyone new to the Bible. They offer features such as guided prayers and Scripture passages, as well as explanations of the Bible's key teachings chosen to prepare our heart for reading God's Word.

Concordances

A concordance is a valuable tool for understanding how the Bible's authors used an original word or discussed a topic. Concordances list every English word in the Bible (except helper words) along with the original Hebrew or Greek word and its corresponding "Strong's number." (In 1890, James Strong created a number system to link the original Hebrew or Greek root word to each word in the Bible. Each number begins with either an H or a G, depending on if the word is Hebrew or Greek.) The printed version of the *Strong's Exhaustive Concordance* has 1,968 pages and weighs over five pounds. Fortunately, it's available free online.

Concordances also list the number of times each word appears in the Bible and each verse in which it appears. Concordances also list the number of times each word appears in the Bible and each verse in which it appears. When using a concordance, choose an edition that's the same translation as your Bible.

A thematic concordance, such as the *Naves Topical Bible*, lists topics in the Bible and all the verses which speak to the topic.

Cross-References

If your Bible has verses printed in the margin or center column in tiny type, you've most likely found the cross-references. A cross-reference is a verse that matches or complements a word or theme found in the verse you're reading. They help us quickly find other verses in the Bible that teach the same truth or principle. Since Scripture explains

Scripture, studying these other verses may help us better understand the original verse.

As we use cross-references, we want to remember an important point: cross-references aren't inspired. The verses the references share are inspired, but imperfect humans compiled the cross-reference lists.

The New Treasury of Scripture Knowledge offers the most extensive list of cross-references available for every verse in the Bible—500,000 cross references. "The cross-references given in the *New Treasury* are not merely to the same word, although that is sometimes the case, but to the same or a related thought, theme, doctrine, subject, concept, or literary motif, even when expressed in entirely different words."[2]

Many Bible websites provide cross-references.

Online Study Resources and Apps

Online sites and apps offer numerous free Bible tools and resources, which saves you money and shelf space so you can buy more Bibles. (You're welcome.)

Podcasts and Videos

Podcasts and videos provide the option to listen and learn at home or on the go.

An Example of How to Use Some of These Resources

In case you're wondering how you might use a few of these resources, let's use some to study the shortest verse in the Bible: "Jesus wept" (John 11:35).

At first glance, there doesn't seem much to consider. The verse contains two words. How could we not understand what it means? Jesus wept. He cried. Done.

But think about it.

Why do we weep? Most times from sorrow, but other times from intense anger, fear, or joy. What specifically brought on Jesus's tears? Who made God's Son cry? And did gentle tears fall, or did He wail?

Since Scripture explains Scripture, let's look first at the verses surrounding John 11:35. The **context** of the passage suggests that sorrow brought on Jesus's tears. His friend Lazarus was dead, which devastated Lazarus's sisters, especially since they'd sent for Jesus before he died. They knew He could heal their brother, but, from their vantage point, He arrived "too late."

The context shows Jesus's delay was not accidental. He intentionally waited to arrive until after Lazarus died so that He could resurrect him.

If Jesus knew He'd resurrect Lazarus, why weep?

Time to do some digging.

If we pull up **BlueLetterBible.org** (BLB) and look up John 11:35, we can click on the "Tools" box.

The **interlinear** links us to the original Greek word in the *Strong's* concordance (#G1145).

The **concordance** reveals that the Greek word John used for wept is *dakruo*, and John 11:35 is the only verse in the Bible where we find this word. Apparently, no one weeps like our Lord.

The *Vine's Expository Dictionary* on BLB explains that *dakruo* means "to weep, shed tears."

Just two verses before this, in verse 33, we see a similar English word: *crying*. Lazarus's sister Mary and the Jews with her were "crying." The **concordance** shows us this Greek word is not *dakruo* but *klaio*.

The **Bible dictionary** on BLB tells us *klaio* means "to wail aloud, bewail."

From this information we can reason that when John wrote that Jesus, Mary, and the Jews were weeping, he meant Mary and the Jews sobbed and wailed aloud, whereas Jesus wept calm but heartfelt tears.

We can now better visualize Jesus's weeping, but we still don't know exactly why Jesus wept. John didn't give us the direct answer, but we might find it somewhere else in the Bible.

When we check for **cross-references** on the free *Treasury of Scripture Knowledge* website (tsk–online.com), we find sixteen verses about weeping in the Bible. As we read through them, Luke 19:41 particularly displays the deep tenderness of Christ toward His people and their spiritually dead state: "As he [Jesus] approached and saw the city [Jerusalem], he wept for it."

The original Greek word in Luke 19:41 is the same word John used to describe Mary's crying when Lazarus died—*klaio* (#G2799). Jesus's tears were not gentle in this verse. This time, He grieved deep sorrow over the hardened hearts of God's people and the destruction to come to Jerusalem because they rejected their Messiah. (This heart-wrenching prophecy was fulfilled in AD 70.)

On the day Christ raised Lazarus from the dead, Jesus had no reason to weep for Lazarus. Instead, He most likely shed tears of compassion for Mary and Martha and tears of grief over the unbelief of the Jewish leaders who were comforting the sisters. Unbelief wrenches God's heart.

Have we interpreted the verse correctly?

Let's check our **Bible's study notes** and a **Bible commentary** or two.

My **Bible study notes** state: "The Gr. Word here has the connotation of silently bursting into tears in contrast to the loud lament of the group (see v. 33). His tears here were not generated out of mourning, since He was to raise Lazarus, but out of grief for a fallen world entangled in sin-caused sorrow and death. He was 'a man of sorrows and acquainted with grief' (Is 53:3)."[3]

John Gill's Bible **commentary** from **Biblehub.com** states: "Jesus wept. As he was going along to the grave, see John 11:28; as he was meditating upon the state of his friend Lazarus, the distress his two sisters were in, and the greater damnation that would befall the Jews then present, who, notwithstanding the miracle, would not believe in him. This shows him to be truly and really man, subject to like passions, only without sin."[4]

The *Pulpit Commentary* on **Biblehub.com** states: "The shortest verse, but one of the most suggestive in the entire Scripture. The great wrath against death is subdued now into tears of love, of sympathy, and of deep emotion. Jesus shed tears of sympathetic sorrow."[5]

Where did these Bible scholars get their conviction of the text's meaning? They came to their conclusions from what they'd learned over many years of the studying the whole Bible—our greatest resource.

We could have skipped all this work and jumped straight to the notes in our study Bible or a commentary, but digging into God's Word ourselves produces a greater work in our understanding and faith.

The Bible Is Our Greatest Resource

No resource compares to the rich treasure of the Bible. Studying God's Word rewards us with truths more valuable than all the jewels in the world. Studying the Bible (the whole Bible) is one of our highest privileges, blessings, and comforts—especially if we find ourselves alone on a deserted island.

CHAPTER 15

DIPPING YOUR TOES INTO EACH BOOK OF THE BIBLE

TO DIVE IN AND fully explain the treasures in each book of the Bible would take a book at least the size of the Bible. I only have one chapter. Rather than dive in headfirst, we'll merely dip our toes into the Bible's sixty-six books.

1. GENESIS

Author: Moses

In Genesis, God creates the heavens and the earth along with humankind to "glorify God, and to enjoy him forever."[1] Tragically, Adam and Eve would rather be their own god than serve the one true God. Through their rebellion, sin enters the world and wreaks a flood of sin in every heart that continues today. The deluge of sin ultimately leads to God sending a flood of water to cover the earth. But God had already set in motion His eternal plan to save His children. He chooses a man named Abraham through whom He creates a nation of people set apart for Himself who would prepare the world for Jesus and His gospel of salvation.

2. EXODUS

Author: Moses

In Exodus, God shows what it looks like to be rescued from slavery to sin, sorrow, and evil's power. Israel reveals how easily we will return to this unholy trio if we don't understand who God is. Through His servant leader Moses, God gives a foreshadow of Christ, our Mediator and the Savior who leads us triumphantly out of slavery to sin and into freedom.

3. LEVITICUS

Author: Moses

In Leviticus, God exposes humanity's inability to keep His law and live holy as He is holy. In mercy, God provided a way, through the sacrificial system, for sin to be covered—for a time. This system and the laws God gave point to Christ, the perfect and final sacrifice for all our sin. Glory Hallelujah for the true Scapegoat who takes away our sins forever.

4. NUMBERS

Author: Moses

In Numbers, God reveals His long-suffering mercy toward His unfaithful people despite His faithfulness to them. Through works of wonders, we see foreshadows of Jesus as the Bread of Life, the One lifted up on the cross for our salvation, and the spiritual Rock from which living waters flow.

5. DEUTERONOMY

Author: Moses

In Deuteronomy, God reminds His people of His commands, greatness, and faithfulness—and their smallness and rebellion. Camped with Israel on the edge of the Promised Land, Moses gives his final words to God's people. He places before them the option of life and death, staggering blessings if they obey God's commands and terrifying curses if they reject the Lord and chase false gods. Moses reflects Christ, the greater Prophet, who became a curse that we may be blessed with eternal life.

6. JOSHUA

Author: Anonymous, most likely Joshua

In Joshua, God drives out the wicked nations and fulfills His promise to His people. Israel enters their rest. Joshua, whose name means "The Lord is salvation," illustrates the salvation and steadfastness of our Lord, who saves us by His grace through faith and is our rest.

7. JUDGES

Author: Anonymous, maybe the prophet Samuel

In Judges, God reveals the stark reality of what happens when everyone does what's right in their own eyes. There's no limit to the depth of evil to which humanity will sink unless God's hand restrains us. Israel's merciful God raises up judges to deliver them in spectacular ways and to rule them with righteousness. At the judges' best, we see hints of our perfect Deliverer, Judge, and Savior, Jesus Christ. At their worst, we see our own sin and need for deliverance and mercy.

8. RUTH

Author: Anonymous, maybe Samuel

In Ruth, God uses an unlikely romance to illustrate His faithful promise to provide a Redeemer for His destitute bride (the church).

9–10. 1 and 2 SAMUEL

Author: Anonymous, maybe Samuel

In 1 and 2 Samuel, God reveals what happens when we long for the world's answer to a ruler instead of faithfully and gratefully serving the one true King. In the tumultuous lives of Saul and David, Israel's first two kings, we see humanity's unending struggle with sin and the wisdom of God's answer in His Son, the perfect and eternal King.

11–12. 1 and 2 KINGS

Author: Anonymous, probably a prophet

In 1 and 2 Kings, God exposes humankind's tendency to descend into ever-increasing sin and ignore God's commands to follow Him. We also see sin's devastating consequences. Through the miraculous works of His great prophets, we see the power and peace that come from trusting in and walking with our Lord and Savior.

13–14. 1 and 2 CHRONICLES

Author: the "Chronicler," maybe Ezra, a priest and scribe

In 1 and 2 Chronicles, God reviews the history of His people (who failed to honor Him) and His promises (which never fail). After Israel's return from seventy years in Babylonian captivity, God chronicles Israel's heights of faith and their plunges into shattering darkness and evil—and one surprising repentance (Manasseh). Through it all, we're left with the stark reality of sin's consequences, the unwavering promise of ultimate redemption, and the longing for the coming of the King of Peace.

15. EZRA

Author: Anonymous, possibly Ezra

In Ezra, whose name means "Yahweh helps," God displays His unconditional forgiveness for His people, which is perfectly fulfilled in Christ. He also displays His sovereign authority over all powers as He moves a foreign king to return the Israelite exiles home to Jerusalem and to personally finance the rebuilding of His temple.

16. NEHEMIAH

Author: Anonymous, possibly Ezra

In Nehemiah, God reveals His faithfulness to His people despite their enemies' best efforts to stop the rebuilding of Jerusalem's walls. God proves that He keeps His promises, and that no one can stop His hand. God will ultimately fulfill His promise to restore His people under the righteous and eternal rule of Christ, their King and Messiah.

17. ESTHER

Author: Anonymous

In Esther, God uses the dramatic account of the evil Haman and his attempts to destroy all the Jews to display sin's power and Satan's lust to destroy God's people, and His greater power to save and preserve His people. Esther illustrates Christ's willingness to lay down His life for the salvation of His people.

18. JOB

Author: Anonymous

In Job, God reveals His sovereignty at work in our blessings and our suffering. He displays that His purposes for His people remain trustworthy even when we cannot understand His ways. Job spotlights the authority and greatness of our God over all creation and the faithfulness and fullness of His salvation in Christ, our "Redeemer" who lives (19:25).

19. PSALMS

Author: King David and others

In Psalms, God highlights the beauty of His people's praise and His compassion for them as they lift their pleadings to heaven. We hear the psalmists herald Christ as the faithful answer to our troubles and the object of our highest praise.

20. PROVERBS

Author: Mostly Solomon

In Proverbs, God reveals Himself as our loving Father who longs for His children to walk in wisdom and delight. "My son, hear the instruction of your father" (1:8 NKJV). Throughout Proverbs, God instructs His children on how to live well and emphasizes the Father/Son connection, repeating the truth that "A wise son brings joy to his father" (10:1; 15:20; 29:3). In this, we see Jesus, the true and perfect wise

Son in whom are hidden all the treasures of wisdom and knowledge and who brings joy to His Father (Matt. 17:5; 1 Cor. 1:30; Col. 2:3).

21. ECCLESIASTES

Author: the "Preacher," likely Solomon

In Ecclesiastes, God reveals the futility of our continual quest for fulfillment outside of Him. The Preacher concludes what all of Scripture reveals—only in the Lord Jesus Christ can our every longing be fulfilled today and forever.

22. SONG OF SOLOMON

Author: Likely Solomon

In Song of Solomon, God displays the exuberant joy of faithful love. We're reminded of Christ, our beloved Bridegroom, and His unconditional love for His bride, the church.

23. ISAIAH

Author: Isaiah

In Isaiah, whose name means "the Lord is salvation," God exposes the sickening depth of humankind's sinfulness and height of our pride. In great patience and compassion, He warns His people to wake up from their sin-induced stupor. In amazing grace and mercy, the Lord prophesies their salvation and ultimately the salvation of all who will believe in Christ who was led to the cross like a lamb to slaughter to redeem us.

24. JEREMIAH

Author: Jeremiah

In Jeremiah, God reflects His heart through His weeping prophet's pleadings for His people to return to Him. But like the Jews who rejected Christ, the people reject Jeremiah's warnings and crush him with cruelty. God, in His mercy, displays His faithfulness despite their exceeding unfaithfulness. He promises to restore Israel, and one day, through Christ, He'll make all things new. All who believe in His promised Savior will receive salvation, a new heart, and live in acceptance and love in His presence forever.

25. LAMENTATIONS

Author: Jeremiah

In Lamentations, God displays His wrath, mercy, compassion, and love. In wrath, He reveals how He hates and rightfully judges unrepented sin through Babylon's destruction of Jerusalem. Jeremiah's deep grief reflects God's compassion and sorrow over His people's unrepentant hearts. In love and mercy, Jeremiah proclaims God's abundant and faithful love for all who return and wait on Him. His mercies are new every morning. His salvation is sure for all who trust

in His salvation, which is found in no other name than Jesus
Christ (Acts 4:12).

26. EZEKIEL

Author: Ezekiel

In Ezekiel, God displays in vivid drama the seriousness of Israel's sin and the stoniness of their dead hearts. A
wave of false prophets in Jerusalem proclaims, "Peace, peace"
where there is no peace. Ezekiel proclaims judgment and
rebukes the wolves in sheep's clothing. He proclaims God's
unpopular—but redemptive—message so the people will
know that He is the Lord. In compassion, God promises to
triumph over Judah's enemies, restore His people into His
presence, and give them a new heart. Christ is the ultimate
fulfillment of all these promises.

27. DANIEL

Author: Daniel

In Daniel, God reveals His matchless power over all
rulers, forces (including fiery furnaces and lions), and world
events. For seventy years, Daniel serves foreign kings without
wavering in his faith in the God who keeps His promises and
works wonders for His children. God reveals to Daniel the
coming of Christ and His kingdom when it will fill the earth.

28. HOSEA

Author: Hosea

In Hosea, God uses the prophet and his adulterous bride to symbolize how the hearts of His people leave their faithful Husband to run after lovers. Hosea, like Jesus, in love and mercy, seeks and saves His wayward bride. Through Christ, the church finds a faithful Husband who will never forsake her and draws her from her wandering ways.

29. JOEL

Author: Joel

In Joel, God reveals that He's sovereign and all-powerful over His creation—including crops and locusts. He's the righteous Judge who judges His people to turn them from evil. In love and mercy, He redeems, restores, and blesses His unfaithful children. Joel looks toward the day of Pentecost when God would pour out His Spirit on His people who trust in Christ.

30. AMOS

Author: Amos

In Amos, God foreshadows Christ as a roaring and sovereign warrior who executes judgment upon sin on the Day of the Lord. The people's sin drew them away from God and into darkness, but Amos reveals that God will one day restore His people and plant them into Christ's kingdom and love forever.

31. OBADIAH

Author: Obadiah

In Obadiah, God displays His love for His people and hatred for evil and evildoers in their exalted pride. In righteous anger, He promises to judge the nation of Edom for plundering their own brother Israel as they suffered in exile and to bring salvation to His people. Obadiah foreshadows the day when Christ will destroy all evil and the kingdom will be the Lord's.

32. JONAH

Author: Jonah

In Jonah, God reveals His exceeding great love, compassion, patience, and mercy—even for His enemies. In mercy, God pours out compassion on the evil citizens of Nineveh and moves them to repentance. In love, God moves in sovereign power over His rebellious (but loved) servant Jonah, as well as in power over a big fish and a shade plant. Through Jonah, God gives us a picture of Christ. Just as Jonah spent three days inside the watery tomb of a fish and was spit out, Christ's body laid in the grave for three days until He walked out in glorious victory.

33. MICAH

Author: Micah

In Micah, God displays His holiness in mountain-melting judgment over the sin of His rebellious people who have rejected His Word. In mercy and love, He promises to restore a remnant of His people from exile into triumph over their enemies. He announces the coming Shepherd-King's rule—Christ, the King born in Bethlehem, who alone can bring peace between sinful people and our holy God.

34. NAHUM

Author: Nahum

In Nahum, God reveals that His patience with evil has an end. Though Nineveh repented after Jonah preached God's message, they returned to idolatry and evil. In long-suffering patience, God announces around a hundred years later that the time had come for judgment. In Nahum, we see how God's patience with evil will eventually reach its limit. At that time, Christ will set all things right and free His people from all who oppose Him.

35. HABAKKUK

Author: Habakkuk

In Habakkuk, God displays a glimpse of the knowledge of His glory that will one day cover the earth as the waters cover the sea. He reveals His holiness and sovereign power over all forces, raising up the nation of Babylon to bring His long-due justice onto His rebellious people. He displays His mercy, compassion, and grace in His promise to restore His unrepentant people because of His great love and faithfulness. He moves His people to rejoice in Him, the God of their salvation, because even when all is gone, He remains. "The righteous will live by faith"—by faith in Christ alone (Rom. 1:17).

36. ZEPHANIAH

Author: Zephaniah

In Zephaniah, God displays His patience and grace in giving Judah time to repent of their evil. In grace, God would save a remnant, judge their enemies, and restore the humble to His great praise. Zephaniah also declares the Day of the Lord when God's judgment would be against the lawless sinners—but Christ is the "warrior who saves" (Zeph. 1:3; 3:17; Matt. 13:41).

37. HAGGAI

Author: Haggai

In Haggai, God calls His people who've returned from exile to finish what He'd called them to do years earlier—rebuild His temple. They'd suffered because they'd refused to obey. God shows He is with His repentant people. He proclaims the latter glory of His temple will be greater than the former. Jesus is the fulfillment of God's promise. Christ is the true temple and our true peace.

38. ZECHARIAH

Author: Zechariah

In Zechariah, God uses vivid imagery of flying scrolls, a woman in a basket, four chariots, and other curious visions to remind His discouraged people of His faithfulness and promises. Zechariah lifts their weary hands and hearts and stirs them action. He calls them to return to rebuilding the temple. Zechariah prophesizes that the Messiah is coming. The righteous and humble King will come, riding on a donkey for the salvation of all who believe in Him.

39. MALACHI

Author: Malachi

In Malachi, God proclaims His final words in the Old Testament and affirms His steadfast love for His people despite their sin. He calls them to holiness and points to the coming of John the Baptist, a messenger in the spirit of the prophet Elijah. He will prepare the hearts of Israel for the coming of Jesus, the Messiah. Malachi reveals the day is coming when all evil will receive their judgment, and Christ will come to His people with healing on His wings.

FOUR HUNDRED YEARS OF SILENCE

40. MATTHEW

Author: Matthew

In Matthew, God looks back over history and presents Christ as the true King of the Jews, Israel's promised Messiah, the Son of David whose kingdom will never end. He redeems the unredeemable and sends them into the world to preach the gospel and make disciples.

41. MARK

Author: John Mark

In Mark, God heralds Jesus as the rightful King and Suffering Servant—both truly God and truly man. He reveals Jesus as Israel's promised Messiah, who came in humble flesh in submission to His Father. With power and authority, He quiets storms, heals the sick, and serves and saves both Jew and Gentile by His death and resurrection.

42. LUKE

Author: Luke

In Luke, God proclaims Jesus as the Son of Man, born of a virgin, and the Lamb of God who takes away the sins of the world. Luke unfolds the gospel of salvation through Christ's humble birth, sinless life, and His atoning death.

Luke records God's acceptance of Christ's payment for sin through Christ's resurrection and ascension into heaven.

43. JOHN

Author: John

In John, God presents Jesus as the Son of God, co-equal and co-eternal with the Father and Holy Spirit. He's the Word made flesh and the Light who came into the world to destroy the darkness. He's the Resurrection and the Life, the Good Shepherd, the Bread of Life, and the only way to the Father so that we may believe Jesus is the Messiah, the Son of God, and that by believing we may have life in His name.

44. ACTS

Author: Luke

In Acts, God sends the Holy Spirit to establish His church through the apostles and empower Christians to preach the gospel and make disciples of all nations.

45. ROMANS

Author: Paul ·

In Romans, God provides the church in Rome (and Christians today) with a detailed examination of the doctrine of the gospel of His grace. He declares our hopeless and condemned state apart from Christ and how we've all sinned and fallen short of fulfilling His commands for holiness. Paul reveals the hope we have in Christ and the gloriousness of our new state through faith in Him. He instructs the church in how we are to live out our salvation in liberty, love, and service—all for God's glory.

46–47. 1 and 2 CORINTHIANS

Author: Paul

In 1 and 2 Corinthians, God instructs the church through Paul on the Christian's hope for transformation and holiness by the Holy Spirit and sacrificial living that reflects the cross. Paul reveals God's promise of comfort in our afflictions and strength in our weaknesses for those who walk in the Spirit, not in the flesh, as well as the importance of unity in the church among the believers.

48. GALATIANS

Author: Paul

In Galatians, God declares the freedom Christians have from bondage to the law. Paul explains how God gave the law as a guardian to keep His people from sin until Christ came with His gospel of grace. Paul reveals the work of the Holy Spirit, who leads and empowers Christians to walk in the fruit of the Spirit—characteristics He grows in Christians such as love, joy, peace, patience, kindness, goodness, faithfulness, gentleness, and self-control.

49. EPHESIANS

Author: Paul

In Ephesians, God reveals the multitude of blessings that belong to all who believe the gospel of His glorious grace. Paul encourages and instructs the church in the power that is at work in them by Christ's Spirit to stand strong against the Enemy through the armor of God and to walk worthy of our calling in the love and light of Christ.

50. PHILIPPIANS

Author: Paul

In Philippians, God encourages the church that even in hardship, the power of the gospel enables us to follow Christ's example and enjoy surpassing peace. Paul calls Christians to follow Christ, who humbled Himself for the sake of the gospel, obeyed God even to the point of death, and is now highly exalted to His rightful place. Paul encourages Christians to stand firm in every circumstance, assured that God will complete the work He's begun in us.

51. COLOSSIANS

Author: Paul

In Colossians, God fixes the church's gaze on the truth of who Christ is—the visible image of the invisible God—and calls the church to walk in a manner worthy of the name *Christian*. Paul warns the church against the false teachings in their midst and encourages them to put on the attributes of Christ so that in everything we will glorify Him.

52–53. 1 and 2 THESSALONIANS

Author: Paul

In 1 and 2 Thessalonians, God encourages the church of the power of the gospel to transform us and move us to ever-increasing Christlike living. Paul instructs the church that even in the face of persecution, we must never give up walking in holiness or give in to false teaching. Instead, the church should excel in love as we wait with eagerness and faithfulness for Christ's return and our glorification.

54–55. 1 and 2 TIMOTHY

Author: Paul

In 1 and 2 Timothy, God equips pastors like young Timothy in how to lead their local church. Paul challenges Timothy (and all Christians) to imitate him and fight the good fight of faith. To handle the Word of God faithfully, watch for false teachers, and spread the gospel despite suffering. Paul encourages Christians with hope that when we finish our race on earth, the Lord will bring us into His heavenly kingdom.

56. TITUS

Author: Paul

In Titus, God reveals the beauty of men and women who honor the Lord according to God's perfect design. He instructs Titus how to train up Christians in godliness, choose qualified church leaders, and guard the church from false teachers. He encourages all Christians in the grace of the gospel at work in us that trains, guards, and moves our hearts to hold to sound doctrine and genuine godly living.

57. PHILEMON

Author: Paul

In Philemon, God vividly displays the power of the gospel to bring total life and heart change by transforming our will to Christ's. He encourages Philemon (a slave owner and new Christian) to treat Onesimus (Philemon's runaway slave and now fellow brother in Christ) as a brother and equal in Christ.

58. HEBREWS

Author: Anonymous

In Hebrews, God encourages the church to continue living in the grace of the gospel as co-heirs with Christ. He proclaims the excellencies of Christ to save and keep us forever and urges the church to hold fast to their confession of faith and not to slip back into bondage to the law. God calls

Christians to live by faith—the only way to please Him—so we can run the race with our eyes fixed on Christ, the One who perfects our faith by His glorious grace.

59. JAMES

Author: James

In James, God displays the power of the gospel of Christ to enable us to live by faith and obey His commands. James encourages the church with powerful truths that grow and perfect our faith and result in good works that overflow from a heart transformed by Christ.

60–61. 1 and 2 PETER

Author: Peter

In 1 and 2 Peter, God encourages suffering Christians with His promises that our trials grow us in godliness. He reminds us that our power to stand firm in suffering comes from the grace we've received through the gospel. Peter calls the church to follow in Christ's footsteps (which led Him to the cross), to reject false teaching, and to live godly lives by the power of the Holy Spirit. He comforts the church with the promise that grace and peace are multiplied to us through the knowledge of God and of Jesus our Lord.

62–64. 1, 2, and 3 JOHN

Author: John

In 1, 2, and 3 John, God encourages Christians with instructions on the nature of true salvation through faith that results in obedience and love. John comforts Christians with the assurance of their salvation and calls Christians to live in faithfulness to sound doctrine, godly living, and Christ-like love for others.

65. JUDE

Author: Jude

In Jude, God encourages the church in the gospel He promised since the beginning and declares that all who seek to destroy the gospel will themselves be destroyed when Christ returns. Jude warns us of false teachers who creep into the church and comforts us with the truth that Christ is able to keep us from stumbling and to present us to God, blameless with great joy.

66. REVELATION

Author: John

In Revelation, Jesus unveils His glory in unparalleled revelation. In cinematic detail, He encourages His bride, the church, to fix her eyes on Him as she waits for His return as the King of kings. John wrote down all that Christ revealed about His coming judgment on the earth when He'll bring

an end to evil and usher His bride into His eternal kingdom
to His great praise.

> He who testifies about these things says,
> "Yes, I am coming soon." Amen! Come,
> Lord Jesus! The grace of the Lord Jesus be
> with everyone. Amen. (Rev. 22:20–21)

DIVE IN!

WE DID IT. WE'VE waded into the Bible together, and I hope you've seen by now it's not as intimidating as its vast size can make it appear. With your toes now firmly planted in the water of God's Word, I'd say you're ready to dive in.

If you want to continue this conversation and find more resources for knowing and loving Christ and His Word, join me on my website JeanWilund.com. But before we say goodbye, I want to leave you with two final thoughts. Reminders really, because we've talked about these before.

First, remember that we don't read or study the Bible to improve ourselves or amass an accumulation of impressive knowledge. God gave us the Bible so we can know Him and His salvation through Christ. The Bible is about Him, not us. It's all for His glory, not ours.

God calls every Christian to study His Word, not so we can master it, but so it can master us and transform us more and more into a shining reflection of Christ. He is our salvation and our source of abiding peace and joy—even when the storms come.

Agonizing trials may crush our souls at times, but the unfading and unfailing Word of God sown into our hearts will hold us firm. Its truths will spring up peaceful rivers of joy and confidence in the Lord.

God will do it. What we must do is my second final thought.

We must understand that Satan, our flesh with its remaining sin habits and tendencies, and the pull of this world will all tempt us to close our Bible and forget about it. They want us to do anything but read and study God's Word. They don't care if we go to church every day or listen to Christian radio so long as we don't read the Bible. God's Enemy and the Enemy of our soul knows we'll never truly know God as we could or should apart from reading and studying His Word for ourselves.

Pray and ask the Lord to fill you with an unquenchable thirst for His Word. Ask Him to give you a passion so strong you'll make time to soak in His Word every day. Then do whatever it takes to sit down and read the Bible to know God—to know the Father, Son, and Holy Spirit. To know God's character, nature, and ways so well that no storm can topple your faith.

Read the Bible. The whole Bible. Don't wait.

Drink deep of its truths and know the Lord.

You're ready.

Start today.

Dive in!

> May grace and peace be multiplied to
> you through the knowledge of God and
> of Jesus our Lord. His divine power has
> given us everything required for life

and godliness through the knowledge
of him who called us by his own
glory and goodness. (2 Pet. 1:2–3)

ACKNOWLEDGMENTS

ALL PRAISE TO THE Father, Son, and Holy Spirit, without whom this book would be no more than worthless punctuation and letters. Because of the Lord—and for His glory alone—I pray this book will help many know and love Christ and the power of His Word more deeply.

To Larry, Bobby, Kaitlyn, Samuel, Ophelia, Brittany, Carolyn, and my whole family: You're my inspiration. My greatest prayer for you is that God will give you an undying passion for Christ and His Word, and that His grace and peace will be multiplied in your hearts and minds.

To Karen Laughridge: God started this book with you over a conversation on a treadmill. Our conversation began an exciting journey to write the book we both felt could bless new Bible readers (or frustrated Bible readers) the most. I could not have written this book without you. I thank God for our lifelong friendship. You're a tremendous source of encouragement and wisdom and a faithful servant of the Lord.

To Dr. Marty Minto: Your help with the theological accuracy of this book is invaluable. Your passion for God's Word is contagious. Every nuance in each chapter mattered to you, and I couldn't be more grateful. I praise God for introducing me to you and your lovely bride Renee. Eyes on God. Pen in hand.

To Lori Hatcher: I wouldn't want to travel the writing journey or life without you. I count it a grace of God that you haven't changed your email address so I couldn't send you another chapter to read for the tenth time. Your love for God's Word and for the English language and grammar have truly blessed me—and thus the readers of this book. You help me better communicate the wonders of God's Word. I owe you a thousand milkshakes with a spoon, extra cherries, and no whipped cream.

To my beloved writing bunch, the Monketeers—Lisa Baker, Lori Hatcher, Jeannie Waters, Julie Lavender, and Elizabeth Brickman: Every day for years, you've encouraged and loved me more than I deserve—and made me laugh until I cried as we seek to glorify God through our writing.

To Pastor Jason Gillespie and all the leaders and members of our beloved Grace Bible Church: I thank you more than you can know. God is using your faithfulness to preach and live out the Bible verse by verse to transform our lives and fill us with a commitment to know and walk in the truths of God's Word together.

To Leslie Bennett and Laura Elliot: You both helped open a door for me I could never have opened and modeled an ever-growing passion for God and His Word. Working in ministry with you at *Revive Our Hearts* is a blessing beyond imagination.

To Ashley Gorman, Mary Wiley, Lifeway, and B&H Publishing: Working with all of you has been an absolute joy. I can never thank you enough for giving me the opportunity to write the book that's been in my heart for years—the book I wish I'd had when I was a new Christian. I pray *Ease into the Bible* will turn countless frustrated Bible readers into Bible lovers for years—even generations—to come.

To every reader: I've prayed for you continually, and I thank you with utmost gratefulness for picking up this book. May God use it to lead you to fall deeply in love with Him and His Word. You will never be the same.

To God be the glory. It's all about Him!

—Jean

NOTES

My Hope for You—Big Wave Bible Confidence

1. Forty-foot waves using the national US measurement scale equals only about twenty feet using traditional Hawaiian measurements. https://ktla.com/news/nationworld/hawaii-surf-contest-the-eddie-returns-thanks-to-towering-waves/.

Chapter 2

1. Genesis 1:26; Revelation 4:11
2. Genesis 1:1; Colossians 1:16
3. Isaiah 14:12–15; Luke 10:18
4. Revelation 12:9
5. Genesis 2:15–17
6. Genesis 3:6
7. Genesis 3:22
8. Romans 5:12, 18
9. Matthew 8:12; 10:28; 25:41; 2 Thessalonians 1:5–12; Revelation 20:10–15
10. Ephesians 1:3–14
11. Acts 2:22–23

12. Ephesians 1:4
13. Romans 6:1–11; 1 Corinthians 15:1–5, 55
14. Mark 16:19

Chapter 3

1. Luke 4:16–21
2. Mark 1:27; Luke 10:17; James 2:19
3. Philippians 2:9–11

Chapter 4

1. 2 Timothy 3:16–17
2. 1 Thessalonians 2:13; 2 Peter 1:20–21
3. Psalm 19:7–11; 1 Corinthians 14:37; Titus 1:9; Revelation 1:2
4. Psalm 119:160; Proverbs 30:5
5. Joshua 21:45; Isaiah 55:11
6. Numbers 23:19
7. Matthew 5:17–18; John 6:68
8. John 17:17
9. Genesis 22:1–18; Psalm 16:10; Isaiah 53:10; Jonah 1:17; Jonah 2:2, 6, 10; John 5:39; Luke 24:27, 46; Hebrews 11:17, 19
10. Ryan Leasure, "Tacitus—Ancient Roman Historian—Reports on Jesus," Cross-Examined.org, October 2, 2019, https://crossexamined.org/tacitus-ancient-roman-historian-reports-on-jesus/.
11. The bracketed texts may have been added by Christian translators.

12. Josh McDowell, *The New Evidence That Demands a Verdict* (Nashville: Thomas Nelson Publishers, 1999), 78.

13. Gleason L. Archer Jr., *A Survey of Old Testament Introduction* (Chicago: Moody Press, 1964, 1974), 23–25, as quoted in McDowell, *The New Evidence That Demands a Verdict*, 70.

14. Alden Oreck, "Modern Jewish History: The Cairo Genizah," Jewish Virtual Library, accessed August 7, 2023, https://www.jewishvirtuallibrary.org/the-cairo-genizah.

15. Frederic Kenyon, *Our Bible and the Ancient Manuscripts* (London: Eyre and Spottiswoode, 1939), 43 as quoted in McDowell, *The New Evidence That Demands a Verdict*, 74–75.

16. Foy Scalf, "The Rosetta Stone: Unlocking the Ancient Egyptian Language," American Research Center in Egypt, accessed August 7, 2023, https://www.arce.org/resource/rosetta-stone-unlocking-ancient-egyptian-language.

17. Joshua J. Mark, "Behistun Inscription," *World History Encyclopedia*, November 28, 2019, https://www.worldhistory.org/Behistun_Inscription/.

18. Clay Jones, "The Bibliographical Test Updated," Christian Research Institute, April 12, 2023, https://www.equip.org/articles/the-bibliographical-test-updated/.

19. John Warwick Montgomery, *History, Law and Christianity* (Irvine, CA: NPR Books, 2014), 13.

20. Romans 8:9; 1 Corinthians 2:16; Ephesians 2:8–9

Chapter 6

1. J. I. Packer, *God Speaks to Man: Revelation and the Bible*, 81, as quoted by Chris Poblete, "The Canonicity of Scripture," *The BLB Blog*, March 7, 2012, https://blogs. blueletterbible.org/blb/2012/03/07/the-canon-of-scripture/.

2. Greg Lanier, *A Christian's Pocket Guide to How We Got the Bible* (Scotland, Great Britain: Christian Focus Publications, Ltd., 2018), 81.

3. Lanier, *A Christian's Pocket Guide*, 83.

4. John MacArthur, *MacArthur's Quick Reference Guide to the Bible* (Nashville: Thomas Nelson, 2001), xviii.

5. Got Questions Staff, "What are the Apocrypha / Deuterocanonical books?" GotQuestions.org, accessed August 7, 2023, https://www.gotquestions.org/apocrypha-deuterocanonical.html.

6. Deuteronomy 4:2; Mark 7:9, 13; Revelation 22:18–19

Chapter 7

1. The word *Bible* comes from the Latin *biblia* and Greek *biblos* for book.

2. The Hebrew Scriptures and the Protestant Old Testament contain the same books, but in a different order.

3. "Works of Saint Augustine: A Translation for the 21st Century." It is in Volume 1 of that series, entitled *Writings on the Old Testament*. Within that volume, it comes from the section called "Seven Questions Concerning the Heptateuch."

4. Colossians 1:27; Revelation 5:9

5. Some Bible scholars divide the Testaments into four categories, lumping the Old Testament prophets into one category and the book of Revelation with the letters (epistles). Only the words of the Bible are inspired, not its man-made divisions.

6. Deuteronomy 18:20–22; 2 Peter 1:20–21

7. "Epistle," Vine's *Expository Dictionary of New Testament Words*, BlueletterBible.org, accessed August 11, 2023, https://www.blueletterbible.org/search/dictionary/viewtopic.cfm?topic=VT0000916.

8. Revelation 1:19

Chapter 8

1. https://www.blueletterbible.org/assets-v3/pdf/dbrp/1Yr_ChronologicalPlan.pdf

Chapter 9

1. A. W. Tozer, *Of God and Men* (Chicago: Moody, 2015), 77.

2. Go to JeanWilund.com for a link to learn about this Bible reading plan and download a free copy.

3. R. C. Sproul, *Knowing Scripture* (Downers Grove, IL: InterVarsity Press, 2016), 143–44.

Chapter 10

1. "Greek Interlinear Layout for Matthew 1:18 (MGNT • NASB95)," Blue Letter Bible, accessed July 21, 2023,

https://www.blueletterbible.org/tools/interlinear/mgnt/mat/1/18/.

Chapter 11

1. See chapter 10, "Which Bible Translation Is Best for Me?," for more information on faithful Bible translations. Not every book that labels itself as a Bible is a faithful translation of the original inerrant and infallible Word of God.

Chapter 12

1. "Doctrines of the Church," Grace Bible Church, accessed October 2, 2023, https://www.gbclexington.net/media/series/qrtx6hg/doctrines-of-the-church.
2. Ronald F. Youngblood, ed., *Nelson's Illustrated Bible Dictionary* (Nashville: Thomas Nelson HarperCollins, 2014), 325.
3. R. C. Sproul, *Knowing Scripture* (Downers Grove, IL: InterVarsity Press, 2016), 25.
4. "The State of Theology," The State of Theology, accessed April 18, 2023, https://thestateoftheology.com.

Chapter 13

1. Matthew 16:16–18; John 14:15–18, 26; Acts 20:28
2. Acts 2
3. Revelation 21:9
4. Bernard N. Howard, "What Is This Thing Called Church?" The Gospel Coalition, May 24, 2017, https://

www.thegospelcoalition.org/article/what-is-this-thing-called-church/.

5. 2 Corinthians 11:2; Ephesians 5; Revelation 2:8–29; 3:1–22; 19:7–8

6. Romans 12:5

7. Ephesians 1:3–14

8. Hebrews 10:25

9. C. H. Spurgeon, "Joining the Church" (Sermon No. 3411, preached on October 24, 1869 and published June 18, 1914), Christian Classics Ethereal Library, accessed March 30, 2023, https://ccel.org/ccel/spurgeon/sermons60/sermons60.xxv.html.

10. Paul David Tripp, *Sunday Matters: 52 Devotionals to Prepare Your Heart for Church* (Wheaton, IL: Crossway, 2023), 2.

Chapter 14

1. Dr. Marty Minto, host, "STEP #2 Truth According to God Part 5" *Study the Word* podcast, August 14, 2023, https://podcasters.spotify.com/pod/show/marty-minto/episodes/STEP-2-Truth-According-to-God-Part-5-e283rf5/a-aa8400k (at 16:16 minute mark).

2. Jerome H. Smith, ed., *The New Treasury of Scripture Knowledge* (Nashville: Thomas Nelson, 2023), xiv.

3. John MacArthur, author and general editor, *The MacArthur Study Bible* (Nashville: Thomas Nelson, 2006), 1573.

4. John Gill, "Commentary on John 11:35," Biblehub. com, accessed April 5, 2023, https://biblehub.com/commentaries/gill/john/11.htm.

5. "Pulpit Commentary on John 11:35," Biblehub.com, accessed 4/25/23, https://biblehub.com/commentaries/pulpit/john/11.htm.

Chapter 15

1. G. I. Williamson, *The Westminster Shorter Catechism*, 2nd ed. (Phillipsburg, NJ: P&R Publishing, 2003).